John Calvin and the Will

A Critique and Corrective

Dewey J. Hoitenga, Jr.

Foreword by Richard A. Muller

Baker Books

A Division of Baker Book House Co
Grand Rapids, Michigan 49516

For Kay

Other Books by the Author

Faith and Reason from Plato to Plantinga: An Introduction to Reformed Epistemology

Happiness: Goal or Gift? Two Lectures on the Relationship between Knowledge, Goodness, and Happiness in Plato and Calvin

© 1997 by Dewey J. Hoitenga, Jr.

Published by Baker Books
a division of Baker Book House Company
P.O. Box 6287, Grand Rapids, MI 49516-6287

Printed in the United States of America

Library of Congress Cataloging-in-Publication Data

Hoitenga, Dewey J., 1931–
    John Calvin and the will : a critique and corrective / Dewey J. Hoitenga, Jr. :
foreword by Richard A. Muller.
       p.   cm.
    Includes bibliographical references and index.
    ISBN 0-8010-2154-5 (pbk.)
    1. Calvin, Jean, 1509–1564—Contributions in doctrine of will. 2. Will—
Religious aspects—Christianity—History of doctrines—16th century.
3. Will—Religious aspects—Reformed Church. I. Title.
BX9418.H57 1997
233'.7'092—dc21   97-25995

For information about academic books, resources for Christian leaders, and all new releases available from Baker Book House, visit our web site:
http://www.bakerbooks.com

Contents

Foreword

Historians' perceptions of Calvin, his theology, and his place in the Reformed tradition have changed considerably during the past decade. Where Calvin was once viewed (or, at least presented) as the sole founder of the Reformed or "Calvinist" tradition and virtually all of the alternative formulations of doctrine posed by later writers in the Reformed tradition were measured against Calvin's theology, Calvin is now understood by an increasing number of historians and theologians to be one among many founders of the Reformed tradition and the tradition itself is understood as sufficiently broad that a certain variety of opinion is not only acknowledged but expected. In view of these changing perceptions of Calvin, the understanding of his great theological compendium, the *Institutes of the Christian Religion,* must also change. The acknowledged breadth of the tradition and the importance now accorded to thinkers like Heinrich Bullinger, Peter Martyr Vermigli, and Wolfgang Musculus press us to identify the *Institutes* as one of several formative theologies. In addition, renewed interest in Calvin's larger theological project, notably his commentaries and sermons, led to the recognition that the *Institutes* is neither a complete presentation of Calvin's thought nor, taken in and for itself, a complete body of Christian doctrine. Reformed theology cannot be reduced to Calvin's perspective and Calvin's theology cannot be reduced to the *Institutes.*

Historical conclusions such as these do not, of course, immediately become coin of the philosophical and theological realm. Books on Calvin's thought that accord to him a lonely eminence in the Reformed tradition continue to appear. And his *Institutes* remains in many quarters an exclusive gauge of the adequacy of the thought of his successors and of the Reformed tradition in general. It is therefore a significant moment in Reformed thought when a work written from another perspective—in this case, a philosophical perspective—points to the incompleteness of

Calvin's thought and the need for thinkers in the Reformed tradition either to find other resources in the past or, failing that, to develop new or alternative resources for the present. Dewey Hoitenga's study of Calvin's concept of the will is such a work.

Hoitenga's analysis of Calvin's view of the human will makes a significant contribution to contemporary Reformed philosophical discussion. It has the distinct advantage over previous analyses inasmuch as it pays close attention to Calvin's text while, at the same time, recognizing that Calvin's *Institutes* neither fully satisfies the demands of Reformed philosophy in the present nor always offers an absolutely consistent philosophical argument. Neither Calvin's *Institutes* nor Turretin's famous "scholastic" exposition of Reformed theology (also examined by Hoitenga) offers a full-orbed Christian anthropology. Specifically, Hoitenga shows that Calvin does not offer a fully developed or, indeed, thoroughly consistent view of the human will and its capacity to choose. Nor does either Calvin or Turretin offer much guidance for an analysis of the civil and moral righteousness of unbelievers. Certainly, both of these issues must be addressed by Reformed theologians and philosophers in quest of a fully developed Reformed philosophy and ethics. These problems moreover look toward discussion and resolution in two very different directions, a philosophical and a historical.

First, inasmuch as it is the approach of Hoitenga's work, the philosophical direction. There is clearly a logical inconsistency or at very least, an incomplete explanation of the problem of the will in Calvin's *Institutes*: Hoitenga has shown this and documented it well. There are logical problems in Calvin's movement from a prelapsarian philosophical intellectualism to a postlapsarian soteriological voluntarism, not the least of which is that the original intellectualism ought not to have supported a voluntaristically understood fall. It needs to be noted here that there are not just three states of human beings—*in puris naturalibus*, *in peccato*, and *in gratia*, there is also *in gloria*. Calvin may be pointing at a symmetrical model of movement from primacy of the intellect (pure nature) to primacy of the will (fallen), primacy of the will (redeemed), and primacy of the intellect (glorified). Calvin, in other words, is quite clear that he assumes a prelapsarian intellectualism and a postlapsarian voluntarism in both of the states of fallen humanity, in sin and in grace. He also identifies the progress of the human condition as consisting in four states. What he does not spell out is the relationship of the faculties in the final, glorified state of humanity. Of course, the identification of the final state as a renewed intellectualism does not resolve the contradiction noted by Hoitenga—perhaps such identification might only intensify the philosophical question. (It also raises a historical issue, which I will address momentarily.)

However Calvin might have construed the relationship of human faculties in glory, his view of the primacy of the will after the fall yields, as it did for the Augustinian tradition generally, the assumption of radical human imperfection even under grace and, therefore, a continuity of the problematic character of humanity between the states of unbelief and belief or grace. Thus, the will in the redeemed state continues to labor under the problem of sin, specifically, under the problem of knowing the good, being convicted by it, but still being unable to perform it. This latter problem, in turn, rests on the Augustinian and Reformed exegesis of Romans 7 as referring to the regenerate Paul—and the resultant near paradox of the good works of believers: viewed in themselves as human acts, the good works of believers as no more meritorious than the good acts of unbelievers. Yet, viewed from the perspective of the divine grace that produces a regenerate willing, the believer's works are directed toward the goodness of God in a way that the unbeliever's cannot be.

In this debate Calvin posed an Augustinian line of argumentation against a semi-Pelagian view, often identified by Calvin as "scholastic." (I note that, here, I find Calvin to be more in accord with Augustine than Hoitenga does—the differences between the two thinkers are more a matter of the context and direction of their polemic than of theological substance.) When Calvin indicates that we are deprived of free choice, he is certainly indicating only that we cannot choose freely between good and evil or, more precisely, we cannot choose between performing nominally good acts in a sinful way and performing them in an utterly good way. He certainly does not mean either that the will (the faculty of *voluntas*) is unfree or coerced in any way; nor does he mean that a person is not free to choose between Merlot and Cabernet Sauvignon (to use an example that Calvin might have appreciated)—or, indeed, not free to choose between committing murder and not committing murder. Calvin assumes the responsibility of all humankind under the moral law. He also assumes that although they know that murder is wrong and that their choosing is uncoerced, some people will nonetheless freely choose to commit murder. The problem is not the destruction of the faculty of choosing, but of the thoroughgoing corruption of human nature including the will itself and its ability to choose. For Calvin, as for Augustine, the issue is that the will itself is captive to the sinful nature of humanity, and that its choice even of the moral good is, in the strictest sense, a freely sinful choice. Calvin denies "free choice" when the term is taken to mean the choice between good and evil, righteousness and sinfulness—he affirms "free choice" when the term is taken to mean that human willing proceeds uncoerced in its selection of objects and goals. He also denies the usefulness of arguing "free choice" in his particular polemical context, inasmuch as such a freedom provides no solace to the sinner. Admittedly, Calvin is not always altogether clear on this issue—he does not make the distinction as prominent in the *Institutes* (but cf. II.ii.7) as he does in his treatise on *The Bondage and Liberation of the Will* or in various places in his sermons, notably the sermons on Deuteronomy.

Given both the context of debate in which Calvin lived and worked and his assumption of the non-meritorious nature of any and all good works, one can understand why Calvin offers no discussion of how fallen human beings can and do will the good or, more specifically, of status of the good as willed by unbelievers. What Hoitenga shows, moreover, is that there is not only such a gap in Calvin's argumentation but that the gap is not indicated by Calvin with any degree of clarity. Indeed, the hyperbolic character of Calvin's argument against free choice (in *Institutes*, II.v) can give the impression that he did not believe that any good acts of any sort could be performed by fallen human beings outside of grace. Turretin, whose work Hoitenga examines as representative of later Reformed theology, is clearer on the point than Calvin: he briefly acknowledges the point that unbelievers can and do perform morally good acts, but then immediately rules the point out of discussion. He chooses not to address the issue, but only to engage Roman Catholic theology on the question of the meritorious nature of such acts. By restricting discussion to

8

the soteriological issue, Turretin, like Calvin, directs theology away from consideration of the broader anthropological question of the nature of human willing in general and the problem of the free choice of moral good in the fallen condition. Again, the gap appears—as does the modern demand for consideration of the broader anthropological issue.

At this point, the historical issue emerges. The absence of particular themes or issues from Calvin's *Institutes* not only must lead a Reformed philosopher or theologian either to seek elsewhere in the Reformed tradition for a precedent or to develop his own approach to the theme or issue. Such lacunae must also lead historians (Reformed or otherwise) first to determine more carefully the context and genre of Calvin's works and second to examine the thought of other exponents of the Reformed tradition more fully. Thus, it becomes important to recognize that Calvin himself did not understand the *Institutes* as offering a synopsis of all points of Christian teaching or even of all issues in Calvin's own thought. Both the commentaries and the sermons offer materials and formulations not found in the *Institutes*. And Calvin's work itself, based as it was on an ongoing exegetical and expository effort, never pretended to the kind of completion that modern philosophical and systematic theologians tend to demand of it. There, moreover, are clearer definitions of the faculties and the nature of their interrelationship in Calvin's sermons and commentaries—and the treatise on free choice against Pighius provides hints as to how Calvin understood the disorientation of faculties to have taken place in the fall. Still, in none of these places does Calvin rid himself of philosophical inconsistency in descriptions of the fall and its impact on the faculties—nor does he offer any discussion of unregenerate willing of the good. All this means, of course, once again, that Hoitenga is correct in his assessment of Calvin's thought on the question of the will.

Calvin's apparent shift from a prelapsarian intellectualism to a postlapsarian voluntarism also poses the question of his antecedents. His soteriological voluntarism tends to confirm an Augustinian and, perhaps, as many have hypothesized, a Scotist background. Yet, had Calvin actually followed a Scotist line of argument, his voluntarism would have been more thoroughgoing: he would probably not have assumed a prelapsarian intellectualism, certainly not to the end of arguing a final intellectualism in the vision of God. Here, as in his examination of the issues of human nature in general, the uncoerced nature of human willing, and the ability of the unregenerate to will outward moral good, Calvin tells us little.

Given the presence of the debate over free choice, specifically the possibility of free choice of meritorious good acts, in Reformation polemics from the very beginning—given also the *theological* as opposed to *philosophical* nature of Calvin's writing on the subject and Calvin's rather strict sense of the boundaries of topics and of literary genre—he intentionally confined his discussion to the narrowly defined theological issue of the merit (or lack thereof) of human willing. Calvin, in other words, had no reason to consider the question of whether unbelievers in other cultures or unregenerate persons within Christendom could perform morally "good" acts even in their basic intention, despite the presence of original sinfulness in all such acts rendering them soteriologically useless. This issue, by the way, is not one that falls naturally within the bounds of a sixteenth- or seventeenth-century theological system (if present at all, it would more likely be found in general philosophical works or in works of philosophical as distinct from theological ethics) given the nature of the theological topic of sin as governed largely by the thematic structure of Romans, the context of polemic over merit, and the general lack of knowledge about and contact with the great eastern non-Christian civilizations.

These considerations also bring us back to our initial point: Calvin cannot properly function either as the sole guide or even the primary determiner or the Reformed tradition on certain points. The problem of modern approaches to these problems or points is that they have not recognized either the broader tradition or the problems inherent in their own use of Calvin's thought. Hoitenga clearly demonstrates—and this is very important to contemporary Reformed thought—that Calvin's *Institutes* offers a rather imperfect foundation for contemporary Reformed discussions of the will. This point, in turn, leads Hoitenga to raise a broader question concerning the Reformed tradition. It is necessary, he indicates, to "go beyond Calvin" for a Reformed solution to the problem of free choice. In fact, many of Calvin's contemporaries and successors did. The late sixteenth- and seventeenth-century Reformed theologians worked to appropriate the tradition and its insights. Where Hoitenga finds the medieval thinkers more balanced and astute than Calvin, I would suggest that he would also find other Reformed thinkers (whether Calvin's contemporaries or the Protestant scholastic writers) also more balanced and astute. Thus, Reformed contemporaries of Calvin like Peter Martyr Vermigli and Heinrich Bullinger, did not understand the noetic effects of sin to be as extensive as Calvin did and they therefore provide a resource for mounting a discussion of general knowledge of the good and of the nature of the morally good acts of unbelievers. Likewise, Turretin and others in the seventeenth century offer alternative views on the relationship of intellect and will and of the relationship of free choice to these faculties. There is also a large body of late sixteenth- and seventeenth-century Reformed writing on ethics, philosophy, and natural theology that has been, for the most part, forgotten and/or ignored by modern Reformed theologians and philosophers.

All of these comments—or at least most of them—point us back to what to me is the central issue of the problematic modern tendency to use Calvin's *Institutes* as the fundamental dogmatic statement of the Reformed tradition exhaustive in scope and utterly determinative of the shape of "Calvinism." The *Institutes* did not function this way in Calvin's own estimation or in the estimation of the older Reformed tradition. Nor, therefore, can the *Institutes* be determinative, on any and all points, of contemporary Reformed theology, much less Reformed philosophy. In correcting this mistaken estimate with specific reference to the problem of the will, Hoitenga's essay points us toward a more subtle understanding and use of Calvin's work and toward a constructive future for contemporary Reformed philosophy and ethics. From the historian's perspective he also directs us, albeit obliquely, toward the broader resources of the tradition.

Richard A. Muller
Calvin Theological Seminary

Preface

My aim in this book is to motivate Reformed theologians and philosophers to develop a consistent and sound Reformed theory of the human will. I hope to achieve this aim by exposing two serious inconsistencies in John Calvin's view of the will, offer a remedy for each one, and suggest the direction that Reformed thinkers should follow in their future discussions of this topic.

The immediate occasion for this effort is twofold: first, my interest in the bearing of the will on the intellect, an issue underlying but largely unexplored by the Reformed epistemology recently developed by philosophers rooted in the Dutch Calvinist tradition; and second, my discovery that a critical examination of Calvin's account of the will is almost totally absent in the writings of Reformed theologians and Calvin scholars of the past half century. I elaborate on these two points in the Introduction.

In chapter 1, I present the historical and conceptual background for understanding the issues that need to be raised in the examination of Calvin's view of the will. This background consists in the difference (and opposition) between intellectualist and voluntarist approaches to the will. These two approaches to the will came to a head in medieval thought but have had far-reaching consequences for modern and contemporary thought as well.

In chapter 2, I demonstrate that Calvin combines (unsuccessfully) these opposed views of the will in his account of its created state. Then I offer an explanation of why Calvin fell into this inconsistency and propose a remedy along Scotist lines, which I call a modified voluntarist theory of the will.

In chapter 3, I show that Calvin has a view of the fallen will on which it has lost the natural components with which he says it was created, namely, its inclination to goodness and its ability to choose between good and evil. This involves him in a second inconsistency that, as I indicate, he himself wants to avoid and could have avoided, along the lines of a remedy I offer in chapter 5. But first I show in chapter 4 that Calvin falls into this inconsistency (in part, at least) because of a misplaced concern to warn against the danger of human pride.

My impression is that the Reformed theological tradition has not discovered these inconsistencies in Calvin's thought but, if anything, has perpetuated them. I have not studied this tradition, however, and would welcome those who are familiar with it to call attention to any prior efforts to do what I have tried to do in this book.

The Epilogue summarizes the book and suggests the significance of its conclusions, both for developing a corrected Reformed theory of the will and for exploring two specific ingredients of Reformed epistemology that have not been adequately discussed. These ingredients are the role of the will in resisting the natural knowledge of God that all human beings possess because of what Calvin calls the *sensus divinitatis*, and its role in the formation and strengthening of Christian faith, the foundational virtue of a Christian life.

Acknowledgments

I thank Grand Valley State University for a sabbatical leave and the H. Henry Meeter Center of Calvin College for a nonstipendiary fellowship during the winter semester of 1995. I am grateful to the Meeter Center also for their invitation to present some of my preliminary conclusions in their Colloquium Series for the fall of 1995.

I am also eager to thank the following individuals who read, either in part or the whole, earlier drafts of this book: Tom Cunningham, Patrick Lee, Greg Mellema, Mark Moes, Richard Muller, Peimin Ni, Clifton Orlebeke, Mark Pestana, Alvin Plantinga, Arvin Vos, and Ted Young. Their comments have helped me improve many of my discussions as well as avoid many errors; the remaining faults, of course, are mine alone. I am also grateful to my daughter, Noralyn Masselink, for many editorial improvements.

Dewey J. Hoitenga, Jr.

Introduction:
The Powers of the Soul

Recent writings of both Reformed theologians and Reformed philosophers signal the need for a closer study of Calvin's view of the will than has appeared for a long time.

While Reformed philosophers have backed themselves into the topic, so that they are now obliged to say a great deal more about it than they have, Reformed theologians have backed away from it, so that their obligation to examine the topic is even greater perhaps than that of the philosophers. In any event, that is the study I have undertaken in this book.

Nothing is so obvious in Calvin's view of the will as its incoherence. Calvin's view of the human will is inconsistent in two quite fundamental ways: first, in his account of the relationship of the will to the intellect as God created them and second, in his account of what happened to the will when it was corrupted in the fall. I hope in what follows to expose the deficiencies in Calvin's view and take the first step in offering the appropriate remedies. Since the faults that give rise to each inconsistency impinge on Calvin's doctrine of faith, I shall also clear up one issue that surrounds his view of faith, namely, whether he has an intellectualist or voluntarist concept of saving faith.

When I identify my topic as the consistency of Calvin's view of the will, it should be clear that I intend to restrict my discussion to his concept of the human will, its relationship to the intellect, its function after the fall, and its role in the virtue of faith. Hence I will not discuss the consistency of Calvin's concept of the human will with his concept of the divine will, as the latter figures in the doctrine of predestination. By so restricting my topic I follow Calvin himself, who said at the beginning of his own discussion of the will: "Here it would be out of place to raise the question of God's secret predestination because our present subject is not what

14

can happen or not, but what man's nature was like [as God originally created it]."[1] Thus the problem of squaring human freedom and responsibility with divine predestination is a different topic altogether. Although it is clearly a central problem in Calvinist thought (and of any Christian thought rooted deeply in Scripture), a Reformed thinker cannot begin on that problem without first having a clear and correct concept of the will itself.

I will not be able, however, to restrict my topic so far as to avoid some discussion of the role of divine grace in the functioning of the human will. Though this topic also raises problems of consistency, I can avoid dealing with them. My main interest is to correct Calvin's concept of the will, which can be done, as I hope to show, without questioning or modifying Calvin's teaching about the will's dependence upon divine grace.

Let me return to the recent work of Reformed philosophers and theologians. Reformed philosophers have been newly motivated, mainly by Alvin Plantinga and Nicholas Wolterstorff, to develop what Plantinga first identified as "Reformed epistemology."[2] In its first phase, this discussion focused upon the rationality of our noetic states, especially of our belief that God exists. That discussion led to a second phase, in which Plantinga focuses upon our noetic faculties. And it is of these faculties that he has now formulated a general theory of knowledge, or of justified true belief, as knowledge is defined these days. On this theory, we are warranted in our beliefs whenever these beliefs are the result of our noetic faculties working properly. Thus the question has moved from the nature of our noetic *states* to the nature and function of the noetic *faculties* that produce these states. Hence the new questions are: what are these faculties and how do they function when they function properly?

The significance of this development in the Reformed philosophical community (and beyond) is twofold. First, it indicates a reaction to the modern prejudice, originating in Hume, against belief in such noetic faculties or powers of the soul. Modern epistemology, ethics, theory of mind, and action theory since Hume have tended to concentrate on noetic as well as volitional states and activities, such things as beliefs and believing, knowledge and knowing, desires and desiring, intentions and intending, choices and choosing, and decisions and deciding, as if these states and activities just appear for our examination wholly apart from their being produced by some faculty or power that human beings possess.

Second, Plantinga's new focus upon noetic faculties indicates a return to the classical and medieval method of examining these noetic states and activities in the context of a theory of the mental powers that produce them. Indeed, the central noetic faculty from Plato and Aristotle on is called reason or intellect, and the successful or unsuccessful function of the intellect is taken by the tradition to depend both on the bodily senses and on the impact of our nonnoetic appetites, emotions, and desires. Christian philosophers and theologians before and including Calvin himself notably added the power of the will, conceiving it as distinct from the intellect. Calvin himself articulates his own epistemological ideas about knowledge, faith, and belief in terms of the relationship between intellect and will. Hence, it is entirely appropriate that both Reformed philosophers and theologians begin with Calvin's discussion, not only of noetic and volitional states, but also of the intellect and will and how they function to produce these states in us.

Going back to Calvin in this way can only help Reformed thinkers resist the modern functionalist prejudice, on which it is assumed that noetic and volitional states and functions can be examined adequately quite apart from the powers that produce them. The modern rejection of the soul's powers and of the soul itself is surely open to question. The common sense approach is that for every noetic and volitional function of a human being there is a faculty of the soul that possesses that function, by which it produces the noetic or volitional state in question, just as for every bodily function there is a gland, organ, or structure of some kind that functions to produce it—for example, the heart, which circulates the blood.

While Reformed philosophers seem to have backed into the topic of intellect and will from an analysis of the rationality of the noetic states of belief and knowledge, Reformed theologians, as I said earlier, have backed away from the topic of our noetic and volitional faculties.

They have too often discussed Calvin's view of our noetic and volitional states with little or no analysis of his view of the intellect and will. This is especially so with T. F. Torrance, who is something of a paradigm of the modern functionalist prejudice against faculties. His self-professed aim in a book entitled *Calvin's Doctrine of Man* is to "arrange citations from all over Calvin's works" while deliberately avoiding issues of interpretation.[3] But Torrance writes four chapters on the image of God in man and two more on "Total Perversity" without a single paragraph on the human will. Indeed, the term "will" itself appears less than a half-dozen times. This peculiar approach is the result of his charge, asserted without argument, that Calvin "deliberately avoid[s] a substantival view of reason"—a charge which he doubtless extends also to Calvin's view of the will. Yet Torrance claims that his aim is "to set forth Calvin's teaching on the doctrine of man in his own light."[4] That Torrance is mistaken in his charge, and hence unsuccessful in his stated aim, will become evident from my subsequent discussion of the extensive analysis Calvin devotes to the human will and intellect.

T. H. L. Parker is more successful in presenting a "simple exposition of the text" of Calvin, precisely because he has "tried to recast Calvin's material, by asking his questions and trying to arrive at his answers in company with him."[5] Parker's account has the further merit of examining these answers with reference to the Scholastic context in which Calvin wrote as well as to contemporary reactions against a "Scholasticized" Calvin. Still, Parker does not develop Calvin's ideas at those points where it is most needed. This is especially so in his chapters on "The Failure of Nature" and "The Knowledge of Faith," in which he offers a minimal account of the role of intellect and will.

Other theologians neglect a critical examination and development of Calvin's ideas for other reasons. Mary Potter Engel wants to absorb and transcend prior accounts of "the problem of Calvin's anthropology" with an interpretation she calls "perspectivalism."[6] It is an interesting approach, for it enables her to incorporate into a comprehensive picture not only the many different themes in Calvin's thought, but also the inconsistencies. On her view, these themes and inconsistencies can all be classified under two overarching perspectives: the absolute perspective of God and the relative perspective of human beings. From God's perspective, "God and humankind appear to be either

17

mutually exclusive of one another or in contradiction to one another"; from man's perspective, God and humankind "appear to be intimately related to one another."[7] By applying these two perspectives to Calvin's doctrine of the image of God, she claims to overcome Torrance's one-sided "relationalism."

But she ends up misapplying her own distinction. On the one hand, the absolute perspective includes the "dynamic relation" between the image of God in human beings and its source in God, while on the other hand, the relative perspective of humankind includes the "substantial" features of the image of God, such as the will and the intellect considered "as constitutive of human nature."[8] But the question is, why isn't the image of God in us, *both* its constitutive powers *and* the relationships between us and God that these powers make possible, included in *both* perspectives, God's and ours? Instead, the tendency of Engel's dual perspectivalism is not to "unify" Calvin's anthropology, as she claims it does,[9] but to invite an opposition between two necessary ingredients in the image of God that are not in opposition to begin with. For what human faculty does not relate us to God? And what relationship between God and us does not relate us to him as substantial beings?

Worse, Engel argues that her perspectival approach challenges the theocentric interpretation of Calvin's theology.[10] Quite apart from whether it does or not, she assumes, without arguing the point, that a theocentric interpretation will entail a "correlative neglect of Calvin's anthropology"; but that entailment is hardly obvious. So it is not clear that Engel's perspectivalism "unifies Calvin's dizzying combination of diverse perspectives in his rich portrait of humankind." Instead, it appears to preclude in advance a consistent development of Calvin's thought, at least on those topics where such consistency is possible.

The most helpful recent efforts in the direction of such a development are by John H. Leith[11] and A. N. S. Lane;[12] I shall have occasion to refer to each of them again. Leith wonders, rightly, about the intelligibility of Calvin's account, but traces the difficulties to "its particular cultural and religious context" more than to the coherence of the teaching itself.[13] Consequently, he is interested more in a "restatement" of Calvin's theology to meet the "actual human experience" of modern people than he is in developing Calvin's thought consistently. Says Leith: "Theology is historical and is formulated in terms of the issues, ethos, and the religious forces of its time."[14] That is true, of course, but it does not follow that nothing more than a restatement is called for. Nor, more importantly, does it follow that such a restatement should lose touch with the truth contained in a theologian's thought, for that is *not* relative to the changing cultural or religious forces of the times.

Lane, by contrast, is concerned about the genuine difficulties in Calvin's concept of the will and clearly articulates some of the issues. He also hints at the possibility of resolving these difficulties, when he observes in the conclusion of his study that

> Calvin's teaching on free will is very close to that of Augustine. Perhaps the greatest difference is one of attitude. Augustine, while clearly teaching the bondage of the will and the sovereignty of grace, took great care to preserve man's free will. Calvin was much more polemical in his assertion of human impotence and was reluctant to talk of free will. What Augustine had carefully safeguarded, Calvin grudgingly conceded.[15]

Lane's observation about the similarity and difference between Calvin and Augustine is right on target; but there he stops. What I argue later (in chapter 5) is that Calvin's analysis of the will can be brought more explicitly into line with Augustine's "safeguarding the will" than Calvin manages to do himself. Such an alignment will make his doctrine more consistent with Augustine and perhaps even develop and clarify Augustine's thought, though I am not here concerned to defend this latter point. My proposal for this alignment, however, will require the use of medieval distinctions that Augustine lacked and that Calvin, who could have profited from them, seems unfortunately to have found more of a stumbling block than a help.

Finally, I should comment on R. T. Kendall's revisionist account of Calvin and the Reformed Confessional tradition.[16] Those of us who have been formed by that tradition believe that it is essentially faithful to Calvin himself. Kendall's intellectualist interpretation of Calvin and the discussion it has occasioned focus mainly on the topics of faith and atonement. Kendall minimizes the role of the will in faith and conversion; moreover, he says almost nothing about the prior question of Calvin's view of the relationship between intellect and will, both as they were created and as they were affected by the fall.

Of course, the right interpretation of Calvin on any topic must precede any attempt to correct his ideas, either about faith or the noetic faculties that faith presupposes. But if Reformed theologians remain preoccupied with expositing, restating, or reinterpreting Calvin, they will accomplish little in the way of providing a consistent development of his thought. So, if Reformed philosophers have backed into the topic of intellect and will by developing his thought on our noetic states and if Reformed theologians have neglected to develop a coherent Reformed view of intellect and will, which Calvin's view of Christian faith presupposes, the time is clearly ripe for a direct address by both Reformed theologians and philosophers to this topic.

Richard Muller's recent account of faith and knowledge in Calvin clearly reinforces the need to pursue the underlying question about Calvin's view of intellect and will.[17] In the context of copious references to the recent theological discussion of Calvin's view of faith, as well as the Scholastic context in which Calvin himself wrote, Muller argues that this discussion, "far from solving the problem of the relationship of intellect and will, actually raises it in a rather pressing manner."[18] Muller concludes that Calvin's thought "falls . . . into a voluntarist rather than an intellectualist pattern," so that, although "faith, for Calvin, is a matter of intellect and will in conjunction," its "highest part belong[s] to the will."[19] Muller's main argument in support of this conclusion is, generally, the "practical, antispeculative character of Calvin's theology as a whole" and, in particular, Calvin's claim that "the will, not the intellect, stands at the center of the soteriological problem: man knows the good but does not will it."[20] Hence his label for Calvin's view: it is a "soteriological voluntarism."

I think Muller's conclusion is correct and easily supported. But why then is there still so much debate over Calvin's view of faith, which is at bottom a debate over his view of intellect and will? Partly, as we shall see, because Calvin's definition of faith, taken by itself without his commentary on it, is misleading. But there are larger reasons. Muller mentions Calvin's "disdain for Scholasticism, not to mention his lack of training in the intricacies of medieval thought."[21] To this point should be added Calvin's distaste for examining those basic philosophical questions that bear on the theological issues that required him to defend a position opposed to the questionable views of faith that precipitated the Reformation. Calvin openly admits, as Muller also notes,[22] that he will "leave it to the philosophers to discuss these faculties in their subtle way" (1.15.7). Says Calvin: "Let not those minutiae of Aristotle delay us here, that the mind has no motion in itself, but is moved by choice" (1.15.7).

But the ancient philosophers found it necessary to articulate such "minutiae," as did the medieval theologians, in order to understand just how the intellect and will function in human knowledge and action. And it is partly because Calvin avoids examining some of these minutiae that he lacks both clarity and consistency in his account. Calvin's antiphilosophical attitude is unfortunate, not only for himself, but for his followers down to the present day, both theologians and philosophers.

Before elaborating on the first inconsistency in Calvin's view of the will, I turn in chapter 1 to the theological and philosophical background necessary for understanding it. Some readers may become impatient with this chapter and wish to move directly to chapter 2, where I begin my discussion of Calvin. I would urge them instead to read chapter 1, not only to understand Calvin in his immediate intellectual context but also to appreciate the depth of the issues involved, which a study of Calvin by himself won't quite evoke. In chapter 2, I describe the inconsistency, discuss how Calvin falls into it, and offer the appropriate remedy. I include in this chapter an examination of Calvin's doctrine of faith, in order to explain both why Calvin's commentators sometimes reach an intellectualist interpretation of it and why that interpretation is mistaken. In chapter 3, I turn to the second inconsistency, which is found in Calvin's account of the fallen will. In chapter 4, I offer an explanation of how Calvin falls into it. The remedy for this inconsistency is so important and its ramifications so large that I devote an entire chapter to it, chapter 5. I close with an epilogue, in which I summarize the advantages of the remedies I propose and indicate the direction in which they point for future Reformed thinking on the will.

The Will versus the Intellect: Which Is Primary?

The inconsistency in Calvin's account of the human will as God created it is this: he claims that the intellect governs the will and yet clearly implies that it does not. Each of these conflicting positions, which lie side by side in Calvin's thought, had already been defended by medieval thinkers for several hundred years before the Reformers appeared on the scene, the former by *intellectualists,* the latter by *voluntarists.* In this chapter, I review the debate in some detail; for it not only provides the background for understanding Calvin's view of the will, but also reveals a controversy that spills over into modern thought and is still very much alive today.

The issue has its deepest roots in the difference between the Greek and the biblical view of human nature. For the Greeks, right reason (or the intellect) is the defining power of the human soul. In a properly functioning human being, reason is the ruler not only of the soul itself, but of everything else pertaining to human life. The nonrational elements of the soul, under the long shadow cast by Platonic dualism, are typically located in the bodily senses, passions, and desires. The Bible, by contrast, locates the defining origin of human thought and action in the heart: "Keep your heart with all

23

vigilance; for from it flow the springs of life" (Prov. 4:23 RSV). While the biblical concept of heart is not always sharply distinguished from mind or even soul, it generally includes our deepest desires, inclinations, and affections.[1] And the latter are closely associated with the will, both its perversity: "He that is of a perverse heart shall be despised" (Prov. 12:8 KJV; RSV has "mind") and its moral purity: "Blessed are the pure in heart" (Matt. 5:8 RSV).

The centrality of the will came into medieval Christian thought by way of Augustine, Platonist though he was in other important respects. It was picked up by the Franciscans and found its clearest expression in John Duns Scotus and William of Ockham. The centrality of the intellect came into medieval thought through the discovery of Aristotle, which was picked up by the Dominicans and came to its clearest expression in Thomas Aquinas.

The issue of the *primacy* of the intellect or of the will, as it is also now called, was focused in two separate questions. First, what is their mutual relationship in human action? Does the will follow the rule of the intellect (as the Greek philosophers taught, when the concept of will is read back into their theory of human action) or is the will capable of rejecting the lead of the intellect? Second, which is the nobler of the two powers, the intellect, because it gives us our understanding and, ultimately, the vision of God; or the will, because it is the power by which we come to love God? A complete account of the primacy of the will or intellect would require an answer to both questions; my present study concerns only the former.

Defining the Will

To appreciate the seriousness of Calvin's inconsistency on that question (the mutual relationship between will and intellect), it is necessary to enter into some of the *minutiae* regarding intellect and will that Calvin avoids; for my formulation of the issue thus far scarcely suggests the important questions that arise from taking one position over the other. I begin with Aquinas's definition of will as "rational appetite," guided mainly by Alan Donagan's analysis.[2] Aquinas's definition is important, for it has its source in Aristotle, takes account of the Christian importance of the will, and is sufficiently developed to provide a basis for understanding the competing theories of how the will is related to the intellect.

It should be noted, however, both in defining the will and the intellect here and in ascribing functions to them in the subsequent discussion, that they are powers *of a human being.* As powers they are not distinguishable from the person who has them in the way one's bodily organs are. Indeed, it is misleading to ascribe the respective functions of will and intellect to these powers themselves; for it is the *person* who performs these functions, who thinks and wills, in virtue of the powers of the soul, in a way that it is *not* the person who pumps blood and digests food in virtue of possessing a heart and stomach. This point must always be kept in mind, to avoid thinking of the intellect and will as centers of activity in us that function at the same kind of distance from who we are as our bodily organs do.

It should be noted, further, that the functions of the will and the intellect are to be understood as a certain kind of *act,* an *internal* act of the soul, to distinguish them from the *external,* bodily, acts of (moral) behavior. The latter, bodily acts, of course, presuppose the former acts of the soul; and the acts of both kinds are properly ascribed to the *person* who performs them. In what follows, it should be clear from the context which kind of act, internal or external, is being discussed.

As *appetite,* according to Aquinas, the will has two main functions or components: it is an inclination, a want, or a desire; and it is an ability to choose. As *inclination,* will is the power that moves us to seek some object we do not at present possess or some end we have not attained, and to do either of these by way of some appropriate means. As the *ability to choose,* will enables us to select either the means by which to attain the end, and even the end itself in cases where the end is one of several competing ends. It is in virtue of these two components of the will that we are moved, that we *move ourselves*, to perform any properly human action; the intellect by itself has no power for that. The intellect, however, has its own power, in virtue of which it does for the appetite (for inclination and choice) what appetite by itself, being in itself nonrational, cannot do, namely, make it *rational.* The intellect makes the appetite rational by forming two

25

kinds of judgment. It judges both what ends are good or desirable and what means are suitable, or perhaps best suited, for attaining the object or end desired.

Will, then, as *rational appetite*, clearly distinguishes us from other animals, whose appetites move them without the two kinds of intellectual judgment just mentioned. These intellectual judgments enable human beings to attain a wider range of ends in a wider variety of ways than other animals; they also enable us to postpone the attainment of ends, in contrast to the immediate responses with which other animals satisfy their desires. Furthermore, our intellect enables us to give an account of our actions (to others, to ourselves, and to God). It enables us to *tell why* we do what we do, which nonhuman animals are unable to do. The powers of intellect and will thus provide the basis for the classical definition of a human being, appropriated by medieval theologians, as a *rational animal*. In short, human beings, in contrast to other animals, can *know* what they are doing (or what they are about to do), why they do it, and whether it is good or evil.

Freedom of the Will

On Aquinas's definition of the will, its freedom is significantly circumscribed. The will is not free with respect to its inclination to move us to seek what is good; the good (or at least what is thought to be good) is the natural object of its desire. For the classical definition of the good is *whatever helps*, and of evil, *whatever harms*; and it is clearly contrary to our nature to desire what harms us unless we believe that it is outweighed by what helps. Now our deliberation over the means toward attaining good ends often yields more than one suitable means, so that we must choose among the means available for attaining them. When we are moved by what we have judged is best overall, it would appear that our will is not unqualifiedly free when functioning in accord with its nature to choose what the intellect presents as a *worse* over a better means; so that, again, the freedom of the will is significantly circumscribed by its dependence on intellect.[3]

On Aquinas's definition of the will, then, the inclination of the will seems bound to seek objects or ends that are good for us, or at least thought to be good by our reason. But the will's choice, likewise, seems bound to select what is suitable or thought to be suitable as a means toward attaining these good objects and ends. Hence, it seems that the more we know what is good, that is, what is to our advantage and how to obtain it, the more we will naturally act in the way our intellect leads us. If the intellect is itself moved to its own end, which is the truth, then knowing the truth about good ends and effective means becomes a necessary condition for attaining, at least in a rational way, the good things we naturally desire. Such knowledge will also be a sufficient condition for the attainment of good, provided that there is no impediment either to performing the right action or to the action having its intended consequences. It is easy to see, therefore, that Aquinas (as so far described) is an intellectualist. The will naturally follows the lead of the intellect in its pursuit of what is good.

It may be thought that this definition of will and its relation to the intellect implies a determinism, even though it clearly affirms freedom of choice. But this is not determinism in its usual sense, according to which our thoughts and desires are themselves determined by causes external to them both. On the intellectualist view of the will, the choice of the will is determined by something within us—both *our own* natural inclination toward the good and *our own* reason, which seeks to know the truth, including the truth about the good. The intellectualist view of the will is therefore a species of "agent causation,"[4] which distinguishes it from determinist views according to which the causal sources of our thought and action lie outside of ourselves, and thus outside of our own powers. We naturally seek what is good for us, but what we think is good for us will depend on what we ourselves discover, or believe we discover, is good; and what we choose to do to obtain it depends on what we ourselves decide to do in the light of what we know or believe.

Pure Intellectualism

Precisely such a view of the relationship between intellect and will invites what I will call the pure version of an intellectualist concept of the will. On this version, freedom of the will does turn out to be something of an illusion. For if our very nature moves us to pursue the good, and we can, or believe we can, find the good by intellectual effort, then knowledge as the aim of this effort becomes the penultimate goal of our lives; its attainment will determine every choice we make. Wherever we fail to do good, it will never be due to a failure of will, either in inclination or choice, but to ignorance, a failure of intellect; for it is by knowledge alone that the will is led to make its choice. This is precisely the view of Plato, who first set forth an intellectualist account of the will, even though he lacked an explicit concept of the will. His account is what I will call a pure intellectualism; for as Plato develops it, the idea of choice, that is, choice between good and evil, seems to play no effective role in what we do.

Indeed, the notion of the will as a separate power is not even part of Plato's analysis of the soul. All that we earlier defined as the appetitive component of the will, its deep desire for the good and its power to choose between alternative ways to attain it, finds no place in Plato's explicit analysis of human action. More precisely, Plato absorbs the two components, inclination and choice, which Aquinas identifies as the components of a separate power called the will, into the intellectual power he calls *nous*, reason or intelligence. For *nous*, as the leader and ruler of the soul, is not only the power to know; it is also the source of motion, in virtue of its *eros*, Plato's term for our deepest desire. Plato's concept of motivation, then, is an *internalist* one; that is, the motives for human action are internal to reason, to knowledge, itself. To know the good is to pursue it. But the concept of *eros*, desire, connotes little, if anything, of those aspects of will suggested by the Greek terms *boule* (will, plan) or *prohairesis* (choice). Moreover, the other two parts of the soul that Plato describes in the *Republic*, *thumos* (spirit, ambition) and *epithumos* (appetite), are rooted in the body; and the body is essentially alien to the true nature of a human being. Reason can rule over these two parts, of course, but only by its knowledge of the good; such knowledge will also be sufficient, however, in making these subordinate parts of the soul the allies of reason during its sojourn in the body.[5]

Modified Intellectualism

Aristotle's theory of human action differs significantly from Plato's and is an advance upon it. Indeed, Aristotle gave us the very concept of *rational appetite*. While Aristotle does not think of the concept, any more than Plato does, as describing a power of the soul distinct from reason, he does distinguish practical reason which governs our desires, choices, and actions from theoretical reason which does not, since it seeks the truth about the nature of things for its own sake. His advance over Plato consists both in his explicit association of choice (*prohairesis*) with this conjunction of intellect and appetite and in his claim, against Plato, that the intellect by itself cannot move us to action.[6] Still, these important modifications of Plato do not depart radically from Plato's pure intellectualist position; hence, Aristotle is only a slightly modified intellectualist. Indeed, his account of incontinence ("weakness of will") can be assimilated to Plato's basic thesis that no one can deliberately do what one thinks is evil.[7]

For a more deeply modified intellectualism we must turn to Aquinas. Not only does Aquinas elaborate Aristotle's ideas, he revises them extensively by taking explicit account of the voluntarism in the biblical perspective, particularly as he found it in Augustine. Most conspicuously, in contrast to Aristotle, Aquinas conceives of the will as a power distinct from the intellect, with acts of its own that are necessary for the action of an agent. The two most important acts, as we saw earlier, are the will's natural inclination to goodness and its choice of the most suitable means to attaining a good end. The overall result is an account on which, as Eleonore Stump puts it, "the will is part of a complicated feedback system composed of the will, the intellect, and the passions and set in motion by God's creating the will as a hunger for the good."[8]

Still, as we noted earlier, Aquinas sees the will as limited in two ways. First, its inclination is bound by this "hunger for the good," because, as Donagan points out, this inclination is not a mere potentiality but an active tendency (an *actus* or *motus voluntatis*).[9] Second, the choice of the will is limited by its dependence upon the intellect to present to it as good the acts it can choose to perform. As Aquinas puts it, asserting the primacy of the intellect in this respect:

> What precedes absolutely and in the order of nature is more perfect: for thus act precedes potentiality. And in this way the intellect precedes the will, as the motive power precedes the moveable thing, and as the active precedes the passive; for it is the apprehended good that moves the will.[10]

The will is not here coerced by the intellect, for the good presented to it by the intellect influences its choice as a final cause. On Aquinas's account of such causes, motion is caused by the attraction of an object, as opposed to being coerced by it, as by an efficient cause. In short, we choose the acts we choose to perform, not because we are *forced* to perform them, but because we *want* to perform them, *attracted* as we are by the thought of the good they will bring us.

Spontaneity versus Contrary Choice

Freedom of the will emerges, on this view, as the freedom of *spontaneity*, as it has come to be called. On this concept of free will, free will signifies only an ability to act in accord with our own beliefs and desires, without being hindered by any external restraint on those beliefs and desires or by any obstacle to the action they motivate us to perform. I will call this concept the *minimalist* definition of free will, for it claims only that actions are in accord with what we want.

But there is another, different concept of free will, identified as the freedom of contrary choice (or sometimes, perhaps misleadingly, the freedom of indifference). On this concept, free will is the ability to act in either of two alternative ways presented to us by the intellect. It claims more than spontaneity, namely, that one can choose *between* two different actions proposed by the intellect; I will call it the *maximalist* definition of free will.[11]

As we shall now see, the difference between these two conceptions of free will is critical to the difference between the intellectualist and voluntarist theories of the will. The intellectualist can accept the minimalist account of what it is for the will to be free (except perhaps where two or more means for an end are equally suitable), whereas the voluntarist (as I use the term) requires the maximalist view, the freedom of contrary choice.

So far as we have discussed it, Aquinas's position is clearly intellectualist; for the will's free choice is restricted to following the best means and end that the intellect proposes to it. But at this point Aquinas modifies his intellectualism still further. He observes that "because the good is of many kinds, for this reason the will is not of necessity determined to one."[12] The modification Aquinas introduces to take account of this pluriformity of goodness is the freedom of contrary choice. This modification opens up, as we shall now see, the possibility of sin. As Alan Donagan puts it, "Freedom of the will . . . is wholly a matter of the non-necessity of any judgment a man can arrive at by his natural powers as to the goodness of an end or the suitability of a means. Even when will seems to fly in the face of intellect, there is always a (foolish, perhaps vicious) judgment which directs it."[13]

The Choice of Evil

But how can contrary choice result in a *vicious* choice? To account for this possibility, Aquinas needs to introduce into his overall intellectualist position a further voluntarist feature that is plainly inconsistent with it, in a way that contrary choice by itself need not be. This voluntarist feature that Aquinas requires is an additional capacity of the will. As Stump describes it, on some occasions "the will moves the intellect as an efficient cause, by willing it to attend to some things or to neglect others."[14] Moreover, "It is open to the intellect to consider [an otherwise good object] under some description which makes it seem not good."[15] But if the object or end proposed by the intellect to the will for its choice is itself sometimes determined by the will's *prior* influence upon the intellect's act of judgment, and in the coercive manner of efficient causation (as Stump describes it), then Aquinas envisions a primacy of the will that clearly conflicts with his intellectualism.

Stump sees here, in the relationship between will and intellect, only a complexity:

Although Aquinas's account assigns a large role to the intellect, Aquinas is not committed to seeing immoral actions simply as calculating mistakes. Cases difficult for accounts such as Aquinas's to analyze, cases of incontinence, for example, can also be handled by emphasizing the interaction of intellect and will. In cases where the intellect seems to be representing something as good and yet the will does not will it, the intellect is in fact being moved by opposite motives both to represent that thing as good and not so to represent it, so that the intellect is double-minded or fluctuates between the two representations.[16]

It looks very much, however, as if, more than mere complexity, there is here an inconsistency between Aquinas's intellectualism, which allows for contrary choice only as governed by the intellect's judgment, and a voluntarism on which that judgment can be at the mercy of the will. For the "double-mindedness" of the intellect to which Stump refers arises from a prior influence of the will upon it, an influence arising from a capacity of the will not otherwise provided by his account.

This prior capacity of the will to influence the intellect seems in fact to be dictated by Aquinas's need to account for sin. To account for a sinful act, the double-mindedness in the intellect must be traced to an act of the will upon it, to avoid any exculpation of the wrong act by way of simple ignorance. In order to sin, the will must not only follow the "vicious judgment" of the intellect, but do so in the presence of the intellect's "better knowledge."

I shall call this power of the will over the intellect in Aquinas's view the voluntaristic crack in his otherwise intellectualist theory of action. It clearly threatens the coherence of this theory. Consider, for a conspicuous example, Aquinas's account of the fall. This account is located, significantly, in that section of the *Summa Theologica* in which he discusses the cardinal virtues and their corresponding vices. In particular, Aquinas discusses the fall in connection with the vice of intemperance (incontinence or "weakness of will"), which is precisely the vice—and this is the significant point—that is so difficult for Greek intellectualism to explain. We fell, says Aquinas, because of pride, which consists in coveting God's likeness. We wanted to imitate God, not according to the ordinate measure by which God had created us to do so according to the image of himself in which he created us, but "inordinately." The inordinateness of "the first man's desire" consisted in its being a desire "that by his own natural power he might decide what was good, and what was evil for him to do"; and "that by his own power he might act so as to obtain happiness."[17] Notice that the evil desire had as its object the power of the will to *decide* what is good, instead of submitting to the judgment of the intellect.

But for us to act on this inordinate desire, our intellect had to attend to an inordinate act as if it were ordinate, to an evil act as if it were good. Here Aquinas invokes the principle that we must always act, even when doing evil acts, under the guise of goodness (*sub specie bonitatis*). Aquinas refers to the principle indirectly in the very article (to be quoted in a moment) where he identifies will as the subject of sin, when he says: "Evil is said to be outside the will because the will does not tend to it under the aspect of evil."[18] The will cannot so tend to anything as evil, for that would be contrary, first, to the very nature of the will, which is inclined to goodness and, second, to the very nature of our intellect, which understands by evil that which is harmful to us. Thus the principle *sub specie bonitatis* is essential to any intellectualist theory of action, since a deliberate pursuit of what is harmful to oneself cannot be rationally coherent. Whether this principle can be dispensed within a voluntarist approach will be discussed below.

The principle does nothing, of course, to alleviate a kind of self-deception that necessarily characterizes the fall. But this deception, referred to in 1 Timothy 2:14, cannot be an innocent mistake of the intellect, for the intellect already knows that one act is better than the alternative act it now also proposes to the will. The culpability of a person's being deceived must therefore be traced to the will, to the power a person possesses in the will to distract the intellect from its better knowledge, thus making the person "double-minded." All this is consistent with what Aquinas elsewhere insists upon, that the will, not the intellect, is the subject of sin: "Sin is in the will as its subject. . . . If the defect in the apprehensive power were in no way subject to the will, there would be no sin. . . . We do not sin except by the will as first mover; but we sin by the other powers as moved by the will."[19] Aquinas does not deny, of course, that sin can also be in the intellect, only that it can be there originally.[20]

But in thus tracing the inordinate act of sin to the will's own inordinate desire, Aquinas seems to suggest that the will's natural inclination to goodness can turn itself away from such goodness in such a way as to introduce something evil, that is, to introduce a *disorder* in the soul where there was none before. Indeed, when speaking elsewhere of original sin, Aquinas explicitly says that "it must be . . . related, first of all, to that power in which is seated the first inclination to sin, and this is the will."[21] But suppose the will's natural inclination to goodness and order can turn into, or give way to, or be supplemented by, an inclination to evil and disorder, even if this change is analyzed in terms of the principle *sub specie bonitatis.* Doesn't that indicate some deeper, darker way in which the will is *free,* belying Aquinas's more typical claim that the will is naturally bound to goodness?

Is Aquinas then still an intellectualist? Yes, because he typically regards the will as essentially dependent upon the direction of the intellect for motivating our actions, in spite of the additional power he gives the will to interfere with the specific moral character of this direction. In other words, Aquinas still takes freedom of moral action to be circumscribed by the alternatives presented to the will by the intellect. He certainly does not regard free choice of the will in any unqualified sense as the *essence* of the will. For that position, we turn now to Scotus, who develops the seeds of the voluntarist view planted many years earlier by St. Augustine.

Modified Voluntarism

As we have seen for intellectualism, a pure and a moderate version of voluntarism can be distinguished. For the moderate version, I take John Duns Scotus as a paradigm. Some passages from his early writings suggest a pure version, for example: "Nothing but the will is the total cause of the act of willing in the will."[22] But Patrick Lee, one of several commentators on whom I rely, points out that Scotus soon moved to a considerably moderated view, which is characteristic of his developed thought on the topic as a whole.[23] Indeed, as we shall see, Lee and others wish to approximate Scotus's developed view to the significantly modified intellectualism of Aquinas.

Scotus is a voluntarist, however, because for him freedom is the *defining* characteristic of the will. Such freedom is also the defining characteristic of the voluntarism that marks it off from the intellectualist accounts of the will discussed so far.[24] Scotus expresses this point about freedom in his claim that the will is "self-moved." Here he parts company with Aquinas, who, following the principle that whatever is moved is moved by something else, held that the will is always moved by the proposals of the intellect. Scotus, by contrast, suggests that God made the human will unique, analogous to the divine will, in that it is an unmoved mover.[25] Hence, as Bernardine Bonansea puts it, "the will has complete control over its acts."[26] In support of such complete control, Scotus often quotes Augustine: "Nothing is so much within our power as the will itself."[27]

How does this concept of the will's essential freedom affect inclination and choice, the two main components of the will? Let us first discuss choice.

Choice

We have seen that Aquinas, in his account of sin, gave the will an ability to move the intellect's attention from one object to another, even from one that is good to one that is evil (i.e., a lesser good, which, if chosen, is evil when it introduces a disorder into one's action and character). But Scotus complicates this picture of the will's freedom with respect to the intellect by holding that the will can even *suspend* its own further choice of any object proposed to it by the intellect. It can do so in virtue of its essential freedom; that is, it is free even with respect to itself.

What happens when the will thus suspends itself from the course of its own choosing to act in accord with its own inclination and the judgment of the intellect? According to Bonansea, this suspension is itself an act. In a recent paper on Scotus, Mark Pestana explains how such an additional act of the will is possible, by invoking the contemporary distinction between first and second intention volitions.[28] Facing a choice between acting or not acting, the will can suspend this choice at the level of first intention; this it does by interrupting itself, so to speak. This interruption allows the will to move the intellect to attend to not just any other good than the one that has already activated the will, but to the very specific good of the will *itself*—that is, the good of its own freedom: both the freedom by which it could still follow through in completing the act that accords with its original inclination, *and* (especially) the freedom it is *now* exercising to suspend itself from pursuing the completion of that act.

Pestana explicitly invokes this second intention ability of the will to explain the origin of sin in more detail than either Aquinas or Scotus do. Having interrupted itself, the will moves the intellect to attend to its own freedom as something good, inferior though such freedom is to the superior good of its simply completing the original act proposed by the intellect of obeying God, as it would normally have done if it had not interrupted itself. In this connection Pestana cites Descartes, who (as we shall see) shares Scotus's voluntarist framework: "I withhold [the goodness of freely chosen obedience] in order to prove myself capable of so refusing."[29]

Still, this suspension is only an interruption along the way of the will's performing a fully completed act. The completed act, in the case of sin, occurs only when the final choice between obedience and disobedience is made (as in the fall). The suspension of the will's normal course toward the first intention act of obedience in no way obviates the choice between this act and the act of disobedience that is created by the new, adverse influence of the will upon the intellect; for the two acts are now presented by the intellect as a choice between contrary alternatives. It could even be said that the will's essential freedom to suspend itself from acting on its natural inclination for goodness is the precise location of the possibility of evil; for if it did not suspend itself, it would not have the opportunity it needs to create the double-mindedness in the intellect that is the presupposition of sin. If the act it now chooses is the act of disobedience, it is nevertheless attended to by the intellect as (at least) the consequence of something good, namely, the prior exercise of the will's own freedom to interfere with its original tendency to act in accord with its original inclination and the original knowledge of the intellect, which would have been an act of obedience.

This explanation of the fall describes it in more detail than Aquinas does in his own voluntaristic lapse; it also reveals more vividly how, in Aquinas's words, the will truly is the "subject" of sin. Of course, it still leaves unexplained *why* the will would *want* to shift the intellect's attention from a known greater good, that is, the greater good of its own perfection as defined by obedience, to the lesser good of its own devising, that is, to the lesser good of "proving" its own freedom through the act of suspending its natural course of acting in accord with its highest good in order to inject a double-mindedness into the intellect. For it suspends a choice arising from its natural inclination to goodness in order to inject the vicious double-mindedness into the intellect. And why would it do this? Nothing more can be said in answer to this question than Caesar said in answer to Calpurnia's question, why would he go to the Forum in spite of the omens against it? "The cause is in my will."[30] Caesar's answer, no less than Scotus's account of sin, exposes the ultimate irrationality of attributing an action finally to the will acting on its own.

Inclination

Once, following Scotus, freedom is taken to be the essence of the will, such freedom will not only affect the nature of its choice, but also the very inclination to goodness that motivates its choice. We have seen how Scotistic freedom includes not just contrary choice, but contrary choice that declares (falsely) its own freedom as a higher good than the good of obedience to God or originally proposed by the intellect. Now we will see how such freedom affects, radically, even the inclination to goodness that motivates such choice.

Lee suggests this latter idea when he observes that Scotus sees this inclination as "only a *pondus or* leaning toward" goodness, not, as Aquinas saw it, a fully natural *act* (*actus voluntatis*) that *binds* the will to goodness.[31] Thus the consequence of the will's essential freedom for the will itself is disastrous: "For Scotus, the will's freedom is identified with an ability to *restrain* its natural inclination (to self-perfection)."[32] In other words, the will's freedom allows it to abandon its inclination to seek its own specific goodness, which consists in the unwavering obedience to God.

Is the inclination of the will so free, then, that it can even turn into an inclination to evil as such? Scotus appears to be ambiguous on this crucial point.[33] Bonansea sees him leaving it an open question, so that he can say of Scotus in his summary: "Neither the intellect nor the object known can be the determining factor in the act of volition, which belongs to the will as a self-determining power."[34] Wolter says Scotus leaves it an open question only in some texts but not in others.[35] On Pestana's account, the will subsequent to its act of suspension could still be determined in its completed act by the principle of goodness, although it might be a lesser good (for example, the freedom of the will itself). If so, then it is still something good, not something evil as such, that attracts it in its defection from God. If acting *sub specie boni-tatis* is a rational principle (as it certainly seems to be) and if Scotus and Aquinas agree that the will depends on the intellect to present whatever choice it *finally* makes as a good choice, then both thinkers seem to restrict the freedom of the will in at least one pretty fundamental way. For both, the will can never be inclined to an evil act conceived as such.

Lee and Bonansea both seek, each in his own way, an approximation of Scotus to Aquinas that assumes their agreement on this point. Bonansea summarizes Scotus as follows: "The act of volition, considered not as a distinct formality but rather in its complexity as a rational decision, can only result from the joint cooperation of intellect and will in such wise that the will is its principal cause and the intellect its secondary but nonetheless important cause, and not merely a necessary condition, as Scotus seems to have taught at one time."[36] They do not, therefore, discuss Scotus and Aquinas as oriented to two conflicting views, voluntarism and intellectualism, as I have done, but as two thinkers who approximate each other in their accounts of intellect and will. Hence their discussions imply only that Scotus and Aquinas avoid the pure intellectualism of Plato and the pure voluntarism that we have yet to discuss.

I have argued, however, that Scotus is a (moderate) voluntarist and that Aquinas is basically an intellectualist. I summarize Scotus's position in two points. First, we are not prohibited by the will's essential freedom from choosing the good rationally, that is, in accord with the will's own natural inclination toward goodness and in accord with the rule of the intellect and its judgment about it. So we are still *capable* by our nature of acting as the rational animals that Plato, Aristotle, and Aquinas (that is, the intellectualist tradition) all take us to be. But, secondly, we are *also capable* of acting *irrationally,* when we follow the lesser good in the face of the greater good. This second possibility is due to the fact that Scotus, unlike the intellectualists, including Aquinas, conceives the will as essentially free, capable of moving itself.

Thus, the turning of the will's inclination from obedience to God to disobedience remains ultimately unintelligible on Scotus's voluntarist account of it, even if this turning away is "explained" by invoking both second-level intentions and the principle of *sub specie bonitatis.* For this turning of the will's inclination from its own highest good (submission to God) to an inferior good (asserting its own freedom) is contrary both to its own inclination toward God, with which it was created as its own proper self-perfection, and to the intellect's judgment that the obedience in which this perfection consists is its highest good.

Such obedience consists in the love of God and the happiness in which that consists. No theorizing or multiplying of distinctions can give a satisfactory account of the defection of our will from its own true self-perfection, which consists in this love of God that constitutes its true happiness. We should love God, says Scotus, both because of God's goodness to us (*affectio commodi*) and for his goodness in itself (*affectio justitiae*). Even if the latter is not clearly a sufficient motive to love God, the former certainly seems to be. What, then, motivates the human will to turn away from its created inclination to love God, the source of all the goodness we enjoy? Even if this created inclination of the will is only a Scotist *pondus,* not a Thomistic *actus,* its turning away from God is incomprehensible. Perhaps the claim that the human will is the source of evil is a mystery, like all the major teachings of the Christian faith, and therefore beyond human discovery or understanding and available to us by revelation alone.[37]

Pure Voluntarism

On a voluntarist view, the will is not only a power distinct from the intellect, with freedom as its defining characteristic, it is also capable of determining what particular judgments the intellect will attend to, in such a way that the intellect is no longer the uncontested governor of the will. Still, voluntarism so defined is a moderate version; and Scotus was not its only medieval representative. There were others who preceded him, especially among the Franciscans, and there was William of Ockham who followed. Together, however, these voluntarists sowed the seeds of a more extreme voluntarism and I want to argue now that such an extreme voluntarism first made its appearance in Descartes. It will be surprising to consider that Descartes, whom the literature typically identifies as the father of modern rationalism, is also the paradigm of a radical modern voluntarism. In defending this view, I take my lead from Anthony Kenny, who bluntly concludes that by actually combining both approaches to the will (that is, a pure rationalism and a pure voluntarism) Descartes's position is incoherent.[38]

That Descartes, in his voluntarist moments, embraces the voluntarism of his medieval predecessors is clear. Like them, he holds that the "essence of the will," as a power distinct from the intellect, is its freedom: "The will of a thinking substance is impelled—voluntarily and freely, since that is *of the essence of the will*, but none the less infallibly—towards a good clearly known to it."[39] This quotation supports the freedom of the will as its defining characteristic.

It also suggests the incoherence in Descartes's overall view, to which Kenny refers. For how can something whose essence is freedom also be *impelled* toward the good? Only, it would seem, if Descartes here means to invoke only the minimalist concept of freedom as spontaneity, on which the free will can compatibly be "impelled" by its own inclination. But it is not clear that Descartes here means thus to restrict the freedom of the will. Indeed, Descartes sometimes writes as if the two senses, minimalist and maximalist, are interchangeable. For example, notice how he moves in the following passage, which elaborates on the concept

of free will, from the idea of contrary choice to that of spontaneity, as if the essence of free will "consists simply" in either one:

> Freewill consists simply in the fact that we are able alike to do
> and not to do a given thing (that is, can either assert or deny, either
> seek or shun); or rather, simply in the fact that our impulse
> towards what our intellect presents to us as worthy of assertion
> or denial, as a thing to be sought or shunned, is such that we feel
> ourselves not to be determined by any external force.[40]

Elsewhere, moreover, it is clear that Descartes believes that contrary choice is as essential to free will as spontaneity. Consider
the passage cited earlier by Pestana: "It is always open to us to
hold back from pursuing a clearly known good, or from admitting a clearly perceived truth, provided we consider it a good
thing to demonstrate the freedom of our will by so doing."[41]

Though this passage assumes that the will, for all its freedom,
is still bound by the rational principle of goodness, it nevertheless implies the same freedom of contrary choice we found in
Scotus. This is the freedom of the will to *resist* the clear leading
of the intellect (which proposes a "good clearly known") in favor
of another good we come to "consider" as good (the will's own
freedom itself). Hence, I conclude that Descartes holds that the
freedom of the will comprises both spontaneity and contrary
choice.

Even so, nothing in the account of Descartes thus far goes
beyond the moderate voluntarism of his medieval predecessors.
What, then, distinguishes him as a *pure* voluntarist? He gives us
a clue in the passage just cited, when he asserts the will's freedom to withhold its assent to a "clearly perceived truth." In this
claim, Descartes suggests that freedom of the will extends well
beyond the sphere of moral choice to an operation of the intellect, namely, "admitting a clearly perceived truth."[42] Descartes's
supreme confidence that the will can withhold our assent to such
truth is precisely what undergirds the radical doubt of Descartes's
Meditations.[43]

At this point, then, we can begin to see how he parts company with his voluntaristic medieval predecessors. Like them,
he teaches that freedom is the defining power of the will, in
virtue of which it can reject the rule of the intellect; unlike them,

41

he teaches (in his voluntarist moments) that the will performs the very operations traditionally ascribed to the intellect. Consider the following passage: "Thus sense perception, imagining, and conceiving things that are purely intelligible, are just different methods of perceiving; but desiring, holding in aversion, *affirming, denying, doubting,* all these are the different *modes of willing.*"[44]

So the intellect, according to Descartes (at least in his voluntaristic moments and contrary to the main philosophical tradition before him), no longer has the exclusive power, if any ultimate power at all, to affirm, deny, or doubt a proposition the truth of which is "clearly perceived" by it; all such acts are acts of the will upon the ideas that the intellect presents to it. At best, reason can formulate and entertain a proposition; the proposition becomes a judgment, that is, an affirmation or denial solely by an act of the will.

This startling claim is nevertheless quite consistent with Descartes's famous statement in his fourth *Meditation* that the power of the will is "unlimited."[45] Thus Descartes suggests that the will's power extends not only to overruling the moral lead of the intellect but also to invading its realm, usurping its power to assent to or dissent even from the "clearly perceived" propositions it formulates. This is the pure voluntarism of Descartes that distinguishes it from the moderate versions of his predecessors, though of course it sits side by side in his thought with the rationalism for which he is much better known.

Descartes also, in this same *Meditation*, attributes intellectual error to the will. Taken by itself, this account of error might suggest that the will is responsible only for erroneous judgments, not for truthful ones. But that does not seem to be the case. Consider what Descartes says elsewhere about *choosing* what is true:

> For we do not praise automatic machines although they respond exactly to the movements which they were destined to produce, since their actions are performed necessarily. We praise the workman who has made the machines because he has formed them with accuracy and has done so freely and not of necessity. And for the same reason when we *choose* what is true, much more credit is due to us when the *choice is made freely,* than when it is made of necessity.[46]

It seems clear from this passage that we are as praiseworthy when we affirm the truth as we are at fault for falling into error. That can only be because, in this passage, Descartes takes affirming the truth, generally, as a voluntary action, a function of the will.

If we take this passage with others previously cited, we can plausibly regard Descartes as willing to extend the praiseworthiness of making true judgments generally to the clear and distinct ideas that for Descartes are the clearest sign of truth. Indeed, even in his rationalistic moments, when he asserts what appears to be a non-voluntarist account of judgment, he goes out of his way to involve the will acting *freely,* at least in its minimalist sense as freedom of spontaneity. Consider yet another passage from the same *Meditation:*

> I *could not help* judging that what I understood clearly is true; *not that I was coerced* into holding this judgment because of some external force, but because a great *inclination of my will followed from* a great light in the intellect—so much so that *the more spontaneously and freely* I believed it, the *less I was indifferent* to it. (emphasis mine)

Though the inclination of will to affirm clear and distinct ideas *follows from* the light of reason itself, yet the affirmation is a *free* and *spontaneous* act of the will. But if necessary propositions are self-evident and compelling to the intellect, as Descartes holds in his rationalistic moments, why does he here feel the need to refer to the activity of the will with respect to them at all?

I have tried to show, not that Descartes is nothing but a voluntarist, but that there is, side by side with his deep rationalism, an equally deep voluntarist strain in his thought. As Kenny shows in greater detail, Descartes can be quoted in support of two contradictory views: both that judgment is an act of the intellect and that it is an act of the will; and again, both that clear and distinct ideas determine the will and that the will need not affirm even the clearest and most distinct ideas proposed to it by the intellect.

If this account of Descartes is correct, he may be as much the father of pure voluntarism, represented in the last two centuries by such otherwise diverse thinkers as Kierkegaard, Schopenhauer, William James, and Jean-Paul Sartre, as he is of the rationalism of the seventeenth- and eighteenth-century Enlightenment thinkers who immediately followed him. Indeed, modern philosophy could be written as a history of the tension between reason and will, rationalism and voluntarism, with the dominance of the former gradually yielding, since Kant, to the dominance of the latter.[47]

The First Inconsistency: The Created Will

The first inconsistency in Calvin's view of the will is simply stated: he is an intellectualist on human nature as it was created, but a voluntarist on both its fallen and redeemed states. Calvin's discussion (in the *Institutes*) of human nature in its created state is brief, just one chapter of 14 pages (1.15), in contrast to his discussion of our fallen state, five chapters of 100 pages (2.1–5), and of our redeemed state, twenty chapters of 385 pages (3.1–20).[1] Although we might thus expect to find three quite distinct accounts of the will, one for each state, it turns out that much of what Calvin has to say about the will in the redeemed state, including its role in conversion, appears already in the section purportedly devoted to the fallen state alone. The main exception is the nature of faith, for which we must turn to the third section on the redeemed state.

Calvin forsakes his intellectualist account of our created state as soon as he describes the fall. He describes the fall, however, in the same chapter (1.15) in which he describes the created state. The result is that his intellectualist and voluntarist accounts of human nature as it was created occur in very close proximity to each other. Indeed, the inconsistency between them occurs within the one single chapter itself, entitled, "Discussion of Human Nature as Created, of the Faculties of the Soul, of the Image of God, of Free Will, and of the Original Integrity of Man's Nature." Let us follow Calvin's own discussion to see how it goes.

Calvin's Intellectualism

It should be noted by way of background that Calvin's account of intellect and will as they were created is an amalgam of biblical, Greek, and medieval ideas. From the Bible he holds that human beings, body and soul, are created in the image of God. The soul is the "nobler part," both because of its immortality and because "the primary seat of the divine image was in the mind and heart, or in the soul and its powers" (1.15.2–3). From the Greeks, but especially from Plato, Calvin sees the soul as the source of life (Plato's *psyche*), which "hold(s) the first place in ruling man's life, not alone with respect to the duties of his earthly life, but at the same time to arouse him to honor God" (1.15.6). Plato, recall, identified the ruling element in the soul as *nous* and the arousing or motivational element as *eros*. Calvin is aware, of course, that Plato's and Aristotle's theories of the powers of the soul are more complex, even as were the theories of his medieval predecessors and Scholastic contemporaries. After rehearsing some of this complexity, however, Calvin resolves "to choose a division within the capacity of all, which cannot be successfully sought from the philosophers" (1.15.6). This is the division into two faculties, intellect and will; it was well established by his own time and represents that part of his amalgam that he owes to the Schoolmen.

Calvin's intellectualist concept of the relationship can be seen in two important passages that deserve quotation here (the first one registers his distaste for the "minutiae of Aristotle," mentioned earlier):

> Let the office, moreover, of understanding be to distinguish between objects, as each seems worthy of approval or disapproval; while that of the will, to choose and follow what the understanding pronounces good, but to reject and flee what it disapproves. Let not those minutiae of Aristotle delay us here, that the mind has

no motion in itself, but is moved by choice. This choice he calls
the appetitive understanding. Not to entangle ourselves in useless questions, let it be enough for us that the understanding is,
as it were, the leader and governor of the soul; and *that the will is
always mindful of the bidding of the understanding, and in its own
desires awaits the judgment of the understanding.*[2] (1.15.7; emphasis mine)

Therefore God provided man's soul with a mind, by which to distinguish good from evil, right from wrong; and, with the light of
reason as guide, to distinguish what should be followed from what
should be avoided. For this reason the philosophers called this
directing part *to hegemonikon.* To this he joined will, under whose
control is choice. Man in his first condition excelled in these pre-
eminent endowments, so that his reason, understanding, pru-
dence, and judgment not only sufficed for the direction of his
earthly life, but by them men mounted up even to God and eternal bliss. Then was choice added, to direct the appetites and control all the organic motions, and thus make *the will completely
amenable to the guidance of reason.* (1.15.8; emphasis mine)

The two passages show Calvin's clear understanding of the intellectualist tradition, beginning from Plato and culminating in
Aquinas; however, they contain none of the modifications of that
tradition which Aquinas found necessary to make in the light of
Augustinian voluntarism.

As to the intellect, neither here nor in the rest of his discussion does Calvin distinguish, as Aquinas did, the judgments it
makes between good and bad ends from the judgments it makes
between suitable and unsuitable means for attaining them. He
finds it adequate for his purposes to affirm in a general way that
intellect as it was created "sufficed" for the judgment of all things
necessary for this "earthly life" as well as for "mount[ing] up even
to God and eternal bliss."

As to the will, Calvin follows its definition as rational appetite,
which we found earlier in Aquinas, and acknowledges its Aristotelian origin. He also acknowledges the two components of
appetite—inclination and choice.

With respect to inclination, he says that the will "in [seeking
to satisfy] its own desires awaits the judgment of the understanding" and notes how "Aristotle himself truly teaches the same

thing: that shunning or seeking out in the appetite corresponds to affirming or denying in the mind" (1.15.7). In the earlier discussion of will and intellect constituting the image of God, Calvin identifies the appetite or desire of the will with the affections, which were "kept within the bounds of reason": "Accordingly the integrity with which Adam was endowed is expressed by this word [image], when he had full possession of right understanding, when he had his affections kept within the bounds of reason, all his senses tempered in right order, and he truly referred his excellence to exceptional gifts bestowed upon him by his Maker" (1.15.3).

With respect to choice, Calvin says that "choice was added to direct the appetites and control all the organic motions, and thus make the will completely amenable to the guidance of reason" (1.15.8). Thus far, then, Calvin's account is consistent with that of Aquinas in distinguishing the two components of will—inclination and choice; it is also as clearly intellectualistic as Aquinas's account, in subordinating both inclination and choice to the rule of reason.

Calvin's Voluntarism

Calvin's intellectualism founders dramatically, however, even before he has completed his discussion of the created state. For in the last section he raises the question of free choice in a short but remarkable description of the fall. He attributes the fall to an act of the will, not of the intellect:

> Adam could have stood if he wished, seeing that he fell solely by his own will. But it was because his will was capable of being bent to one side or another, and was not given the constancy to persevere, that he fell so easily. Yet his choice was free, and not that alone, but the highest rectitude was in his mind and will, and all the organic parts were rightly composed to obedience, until in destroying himself he corrupted his own blessings. (1.15.8)

Here Calvin clearly undermines the intellectualist account he has just given, in the very same section. For he attributes the fall not to a failure of the intellect, but to the free choice of the will. That is, the will was free *not* "always to be mindful of the bidding of the understanding" (to quote his earlier intellectualist language 1.15.7); *not* to be "completely amenable to the guidance of reason" (1.15.8).

Freedom of the Will

If the will was created "capable of being bent to one side or the other," it possesses a freedom not hinted at in the two earlier intellectualist accounts, a freedom of contrary choice with respect to good and evil. Elsewhere Calvin extends this contrariety to the inclination of the will: "We admit that man's condition while he still remained upright was such that he could incline to either side" (2.3.10). The spontaneity of the will's inclination is assumed, of course: "Man, as he was corrupted by the Fall, sinned willingly, not unwillingly or by compulsion; by the most eager inclination of his heart, not by forced compulsion; by the prompting of his own lust, not by compulsion from without" (2.3.5). These passages taken together imply (at least) a modified voluntarism, as I defined that position in chapter 1; for in the fall, as Calvin here describes it, the will demonstrates its essential freedom from the rule of the intellect, both in its inclination and in its choice. But nothing of this contrary freedom of the will was even hinted at in the passages quoted earlier; indeed, their entire thrust was that the will would "choose and follow what the understanding pronounces good" and "reject and flee what it disapproves." Again, there "the will is always mindful of the bidding of the understanding, and in its desires awaits the judgment of the understanding." And again, "Then was choice added, to direct the appetites . . . and thus make the will completely amenable to the guidance of reason."[3] Calvin's sudden move from an intellectualist account of the will to a voluntarist account of it recalls Aquinas's voluntarist lapse from his otherwise intellectualistic theory of the will; it is noteworthy that the occasion is similar in both cases: the need to account for sin.[4]

Like Aquinas, Calvin also ascribes to the will an ability to avert the attention of the intellect from its better knowledge. Although Calvin does not make a point of this ability in 1.15.8, where he discusses the fall, elsewhere (notably right at the beginning of the *Institutes*) he is very explicit about this power of the will. Having there just delineated his doctrine of an immediate, "naturally inborn" knowledge of God (the *sensus divinitatis*), he observes that fallen human beings try to "efface" or "blot out" this knowledge. Thus the will resists the better knowledge of the intellect for its own purpose of excusing the sinner from divine judgment (1.4). Thus Calvin is as keenly aware as Aquinas that the will, not the intellect, must be the "subject of sin."

His voluntarism is also explicit in his rejection, in Book II, of Plato's doctrine that wrongdoing is due to ignorance. Indeed, he even suggests that Plato's intellectualism is itself a veritable example of the willful aversion of the human mind from its better knowledge whereby the sinfulness of our fallen condition stands condemned: "Man is so indulgent toward himself that when he commits evil he readily averts his mind, as much as he can, from the feeling of sin. This is why Plato seems to have been compelled to consider (in his *Protagoras*) that we sin only out of ignorance" (2.2.22). But these efforts of the will are without complete success: "The sinner tries to evade his innate power to judge between good and evil. Still, he is continually drawn back to it, and is not so much as permitted to wink at it without being forced, whether he will or not, at times to open his eyes" (2.2.22). The voluntarism that motivates Calvin's criticism of Plato here is unmistakable.

It should not be thought, however, that the strength of intellect to persist in its better knowledge even in the fallen state (1.4) implies its primacy over the will; for the point relevant to the issue of primacy is precisely the freedom of the will to turn away from this better knowledge retained by the intellect. Only such primacy of the will can explain the possibility of the fall in the first place in such a way that Calvin can ascribe full responsibility to human beings both for the fall itself and its consequences in the fallen state (a topic to which we return when we discuss the second, different kind of inconsistency in chapter 3).

Hence, Calvin's earlier intellectualist account of the will in its created state must be mistaken. That account of the will as created is also inconsistent with his clearly voluntarist accounts of the fallen and redeemed states, with what Richard Muller calls

Calvin's "soteriological voluntarism." Let us now turn to that account.

Calvin's Soteriological Voluntarism

While it is relatively simple to expose the inconsistency between Calvin's intellectualism and his voluntarism in the short portion (14 pages) he devotes to human nature as it was created, it is necessary to read the disproportionately long portions devoted to the fallen state (100 pages) and to the redeemed state (385 pages) in their entirety to determine that Calvin indeed thoroughly abandons the intellectualism that characterizes his initial account of the will as it was created. But that is indeed what he does. I shall be content here only to cite a few passages that summarize the voluntarism that permeates the entire account of both states. As earlier noted, Calvin continually anticipates the redeemed state in his discussion of the fallen state, except for the topic of faith. In fact, his discussion of the redeemed state of the will, and of the intellect particularly, is more complete in the former portion than in the latter; thus the essence of his voluntarism for the fallen state can be found in just two chapters (2.2.26–27) and for conversion in nine more (2.3.6–14). Except for faith, therefore, I will here present Calvin's voluntarism for both states from those chapters just identified.

The voluntarism in Calvin's delineation of the fallen state is intimately connected to his doctrine of the bondage of the will; in fact, as we shall see later, the second inconsistency in Calvin's view of the will stems from his overreaching himself in elaborating that doctrine. I mention it here only because Calvin refers to it in one of the more explicit statements of his voluntarist conception of the will in the fallen state. In that statement Calvin explicitly identifies the will, not the intellect, as the "chief seat" of the power of sin: "But if the whole man lies under the power of sin, surely it is necessary that the will, which is its chief seat, be restrained by the stoutest bonds" (2.2.27). These bonds, Calvin goes on to explain, prevent the will from taking even the first step of "preparing" itself for the restorative power of grace.

Turning to conversion, Calvin is equally clear that it too orig-inates in the will, just like the fall into sin that made it necessary for redemption. Commenting on Philippians 1:6, Calvin says that Paul "denotes the very origin of conversion itself, which is in the will. God begins his good work in us, therefore, by arousing love and desire and zeal for righteousness in our hearts; or to speak more correctly, by bending, forming, and directing, our hearts to righteousness" (2.3.6). Notice that Calvin not only locates the origin of conversion in the will, but also emphasizes that it is the appetitive component of the will that needs to be changed, more so than its power of choice. When (and only when) the inclina-tion of the will is "wholly transformed and renewed" by grace (not just "strengthened") can the will once again "aspire effec-tively to the choice of good" (2.3.6). Thus Calvin focuses upon the will as the center of the fallen person's transformation by grace. These quotations and Calvin's elaboration, over the eight following sections (7–14), of the points they contain firmly estab-lish his "soteriological voluntarism."

Faith

It would be easy on first reading Calvin's famous definition of faith to conclude, in spite of the voluntarism that permeates his discussion of the fallen state and of conversion, that he is never-theless an intellectualist on the nature of faith. For what could more clearly suggest the primacy of the intellect than a defini-tion of faith as knowledge itself? Says Calvin:

> Now we shall possess a right definition of faith if we call it a firm and certain knowledge of God's benevolence toward us, founded upon the truth of the freely given promise in Christ, both revealed to our minds and sealed upon our hearts through the Holy Spirit. (3.2.7)

Add to this definition such statements as the following that we find in the context of this definition, such as: "Faith rests not on ignorance, but on knowledge" (3.2.2) and "faith rests upon the knowledge of Christ" (3.2.8), and an intellectualist conclusion with respect to Calvin's concept of faith seems unavoidable.

Even Paul Helm, at one point in his otherwise careful critique of Kendall's intellectualist interpretation of Calvin, is led by the passage just cited from 3.2.2 to suggest a primacy of the intellect in Calvin's doctrine of conversion:

> So according to Calvin, in conversion the mind is renewed to appreciate the message of the Cross and to apprehend the promise by Spirit-given faith, and the will is renewed in such a way that the person turns to God in consecration and obedience. In this process primacy attaches to the mind. ("Faith rests not on ignorance, but on knowledge.") It is the mind that apprehends the good news, and the newly-empowered will responds.[5] (p. 56; the quotation is from 3.2.2)

I believe that Helm has been misled by this passage. The reason is this: this passage and the other one quoted above are found in two highly polemical sections. In one of these (which precedes his definition) Calvin disputes a mistaken notion of "implicit faith" (3.2.2–5); in the other (which follows his definition), he disputes what he calls "that worthless distinction between formed and unformed faith which is tossed about the schools" (3.2.8; see 9–13). Calvin develops his definition of faith in two sections (6–7) that immediately separate these two polemical sections. This placement of his definition is unfortunate, not only for the reader who reads the chapter on faith (3.2) with the intellectualist/voluntarist issue in mind but also for Calvin himself since, it could be argued, and I will argue, it is only these polemics that lead him to give what appears to be an *intellectualist shape* to his definition of faith.

If Calvin really does have an intellectualist concept of faith, however, his teaching will be even more inconsistent than I have already portrayed it. Not only would he have moved from an intellectualist concept of the will for the created state to a voluntarist one for the fall, the fallen state, and conversion, but he would then have moved back again to an intellectualist position on faith, which is at the center of conversion and the converted life. Fortunately, however, there is sufficient, even if not completely unambiguous, evidence that the intellectualism of Calvin's definition of faith is only an appearance. This may be shown, first, from an analysis of the definition itself, then from the immediate context leading up to it, and finally from Calvin's own lengthy commentary on it, later in the chapter (sections 14–37), following all the polemics.

The Definition and Its Context

Although Calvin identifies faith as knowledge at the beginning of the definition, at the end he refers to the mind and heart working *together*. By "heart," recall, Calvin generally means "will"; and what Calvin claims at the end of the definition is that the knowledge of faith is "both revealed to our minds and sealed upon our hearts through the Holy Spirit" (3.2.7). This language implies that intellect and heart are at least *equally* involved in faith, so that nothing in the definition itself will support a *primacy* of the intellect.

Indeed, this equal role of the intellect and will is the point Calvin makes in the immediate context of his definition: "Therefore our mind must be otherwise illumined and our heart strengthened, that the Word of God may obtain full faith among us" (3.2.7). This point, together with the definition itself, constitutes the climax of the two sections, 6 and 7, in which Calvin takes leave from the first polemic (against implicit faith) for the purpose, apparently, of formulating his definition of faith, before continuing his second polemic (against the distinction between formed and unformed faith).

A review of the earlier polemic suggests that it is this polemic that shapes Calvin's definition of faith as knowledge. Still, it is also clear that Calvin heads off an intellectualist interpretation of that definition. Not that he is doing this consciously, with the intellectualist- voluntarist issue in mind; for though the issue had been formulated and disputed for centuries before his time, Calvin nowhere addresses the issue as such, either in his polemical or in his constructive discussions. His polemic against implicit faith as interpreted by some of the "Schoolmen" addresses a narrower topic, namely, that in reducing faith to "reverence for the church" these Schoolmen ignore the essential role of knowledge in true faith. He does not deny a proper sense of "implicit faith," on which "most things are now implicit for us, and will be so until, laying aside the weight of the flesh, we come nearer to the presence of God" (3.2.3). What he denies is the view that "believing means to understand nothing, provided only that you submit your feeling obediently to the church" (3.2.2). Hence his assertion, picked up by Helm, that "faith rests not on ignorance, but on knowledge."

But the questions raised by this polemic are, what is the nature of this knowledge? and what does Calvin mean when he says that faith "rests on" it? The knowledge Calvin insists on as an ingredient in faith is this: "For faith consists in the knowledge of God and Christ, not in reverence for the church" (3.2.3). This knowledge is dependent on accepting Scripture as a revelation from God himself: "we must be reminded that there is a permanent relationship between faith and the Word" (3.2.6). In other words, the role of the church is to bring us to hear God himself speak to us; it may not stand between us and God as the object of our faith. Faith is, as the definition presently claims, "a firm and certain knowledge of God's benevolence toward us," which is a knowledge we possess not on the say-so of the church, but on the authority of God himself, who speaks to us in Scripture.

However, to affirm that such knowledge is a necessary ingredient in faith is not to affirm that faith *rests on* it, as an intellectualist account would require. What faith rests on is the revelation, the Word of God: "The same Word is the basis whereby faith is supported and sustained; if it turns away from the Word it falls" (3.2.6). All Calvin means here is that the knowledge offered in revelation is *presupposed* as the objective content of faith, which must be appropriated by the will but can also be resisted by it. For the context suggests that the turning of the mind either to or away from this content will be an activity of the heart, the will. Both components of the will—inclination and choice—are involved when God seeks our response to his offer of salvation: "He always represents himself through his Word to those whom he wills to *draw* to himself. For that reason, Paul defines faith as that *obedience* which is given to the gospel [Romans 1:5]" (3.2.6; emphasis mine). That God *draws* us to himself suggests that he offers us something good, something that will appeal to the inclination of our wills; and our *accepting* this good is an act of obedience, which implies a choice of the will, required to obtain this good. Thus an act of will is as necessary a part of faith as an act of intellect. That is why Calvin presently concludes his definition as he does, affirming that the knowledge of faith must also be "sealed upon our hearts through the Holy Spirit." Of course, neither the knowledge nor the inclination and choice is possible without a divine illumination for the former and the Holy Spirit's strengthening of the will for the latter.

The context preceding Calvin's definition of faith contains further ideas that imply the deep involvement of the will. "So long as your mind is at war with itself, the Word will be of doubtful and weak authority, or rather of none" (3.2.6). This language recalls the double-mindedness which, as we saw earlier, Aquinas accounts for by tracing it to an activity of the will, when it moves the intellect to attend to some lower good besides a higher good. In conversion, as Calvin points out, the problem of double-mindedness is created by the fact that God reveals himself to the mind both in his justice, by which our evil doing should be punished, and in his mercy, by which he forgives us:

> But since man's heart is not aroused to faith at every word of God, we must find out at this point what, strictly speaking, faith looks to in the Word. . . . Where our conscience sees only indignation and vengeance, how can it fail to tremble and be afraid? or to shun the God whom it dreads? Yet faith ought to seek God, not to shun him. (3.2.7)

Here again Calvin uses the language of obligation: faith *ought* to seek God, not shun him. But faith can do this only if the mind is concentrated on divine benevolence and mercy, not divine "indignation and vengeance." The mind can do this only by an inclination of the will that is *attracted* by divine goodness: "Thus, surely, we shall more closely approach the nature of faith; for it is after we have learned that our salvation rests with God that we are attracted to seek him" (3.2.7). How can the inclination of our will be attracted to the grace of the gospel, not its judgment? Only if our will *directs* the attention of our minds to the "promise of grace, which can testify to us that the Father is merciful; since we can approach him in no other way, and upon grace alone the heart of man can rest" (3.2.7).

It may be thought that there is a trace of intellectualism in Calvin's saying here that "it is after we have learned that salvation rests with God that we are attracted to seek him." Doesn't this sound as if Calvin assumes that the attraction of the will naturally follows upon the judgment of the intellect, in this case a judgment "learned" from the gospel? Not necessarily, for nothing in what I have called moderate voluntarism *prevents* the will from following the lead of the intellect, as described here; what it requires is only that the will also be able to *resist* that lead and even turn away from it. As we shall see presently, the will of the believer can resist some of the truth it learns from the gospel, when the struggle of the soul is between faith and unbelief.

By invoking the relationship between will and intellect as Aquinas defines it (chapter 1), I now have been able to make explicit the role of the will, which is only implicit in Calvin's own text. My point in so doing is to show that Calvin concludes his definition with a reference to the heart precisely because he does not have an intellectualist concept of faith. He does not believe, in the intellectualist language he himself used originally to describe our nature as it was created, that the will *always* follows the leading of the intellect. Indeed, when in conversion the intellect is illumined by the Word and the Spirit, the will must be "strengthened" or "sealed" in such a way that the promise of grace outweighs the judgment upon our sin, which is also present in our minds; for the gospel of forgiveness is embedded in a revelation of divine judgment that only intensifies the sense of sin we may already have possessed apart from that revelation. "The knowledge of God's goodness will not be held very important unless it makes us rely on that goodness. . . . Therefore our mind must be otherwise illumined and our heart strengthened, that the Word of God may obtain full faith among us" (3.2.2).

Faith: Lost and Regained

Here it will be instructive to digress briefly and elaborate on a comparison between conversion and the fall with respect to the will and the intellect. First, it is striking to note that Calvin not only regards the presence of faith as the *beginning* of conversion, but also its loss as the *root* of the fall: "Since the woman through unfaithfulness was led away from God's Word by the serpent's deceit, it is already clear that disobedience was the beginning of the Fall. . . . Unfaithfulness, then, was the root of the Fall" (2.1.4). The parallel between loss of faith in the fall and its recovery in conversion requires, it would seem, a parallel account of the role of will in each. We can now point out that parallel. Just as we earlier saw that Calvin had to abandon his intellectualism to account for the fall, so here we see that Calvin cannot return to such an intellectualism in his account of faith. For just as disobedience (by which in the fall Adam faithlessly "revolted from God's authority" and "because, contemptuous of truth, he turned aside to falsehood" [2.1.4]) requires a voluntarist account of unfaithfulness because it is "contemptuous of truth," so obedience to the gospel (by which in conversion believers believe its authority and turn back to God's love) requires a voluntarist account of faith. That is just what we should expect if Calvin is to have a consistent account of the will for each.

Still, our analysis so far of Calvin's definition of faith and the polemical context preceding it shows only that will and intellect are equally involved in faith. While this equality is sufficient to head off an intellectualist interpretation of Calvin's definition of faith, it does not yet establish a voluntarist one. For all that we have discovered so far, Calvin's account of the will and intellect in faith yields no more than Stump's noncommittal account of Aquinas's teaching "that the will is part of a complicated feedback system composed of the will, the intellect, and the passion and set in motion by God's creating the will as a hunger for the good."[6] Just as we saw, however, that Aquinas has to forsake so delicate a balance between will and intellect (let alone the primacy of intellect that typically characterizes his approach) for a primacy of the will when he has to explain the fall, and that Calvin likewise has to abandon his explicitly intellectualistic account of the created state, so it would be most surprising to find Calvin now reverting to an intellectualist account of faith. But does he go further and tilt the balance between intellect and will so far described in favor of the will? In Muller's phrase, is it clear that Calvin is consistently a "soteriological voluntarist," particularly with respect to faith, the very first step in conversion? Is Muller correct when he claims that "faith, for Calvin, is a matter of the intellect and will in conjunction—with the highest part, not merely the instrumental part, of faith belonging to the will"?[7]

Calvin's Commentary on His Definition of Faith

The answer to these questions is yes, Calvin does eventually tilt the balance between intellect and will in the direction of the will's being the "highest part" of faith. To see that this is so, we must turn to his commentary on the definition; it follows the second polemical section, which immediately succeeds the definition.

The first thing Calvin does in this commentary is to distinguish between the knowledge of faith and ordinary intellectual comprehension: "When we call faith knowledge, we do not mean comprehension of the sort that is commonly concerned with those things which fall under human sense perception" (3.2.14). Here (as elsewhere, for example, section 41) Calvin appeals to the common sense distinction between seeing and believing, on which to believe is to precisely not see an object (either with the senses or the intellect) but to accept that object on the testimony of another. Thus he cites St. Paul: "While dwelling in this body, we wander from the Lord, for we walk by faith, not sight [2 Corinthians 5:6–7]" and comments as follows: "By these words he shows that those things which we know through faith are nonetheless absent from us and go unseen. From this we conclude that the knowledge of faith consists in assurance rather than comprehension" (3.2.14). By defining the knowledge of faith as assurance, he directly injects a noncognitive component into the intellectual element of faith; for "assurance" connotes much more a feeling of the heart and, perhaps we may also say, an attitude of the will.[8]

Though Calvin does not add "of the heart" here to "assurance," he refers to the heart in the very next paragraph; the passage is worth quoting in full, since it opposes the assurance of faith to unbelief:

> We add the words "sure and firm" [to "knowledge" in the definition] in order to express a more solid constancy of persuasion. For, as faith is not content with a doubtful and changeable opinion, so is it not content with an obscure and confused concep-

tion; but requires full and fixed certainty, such as men are wont
to have from things experienced and proved. For unbelief is so
deeply rooted in our hearts, and we are so inclined to it, that not
without hard struggle is each one able to persuade himself of what
all confess with the mouth: namely, that God is faithful. (3.2.15)

Notice the amazing candor with which Calvin assumes that faith
and unbelief, and the struggle between them, coexist in the hearts,
that is, the wills of believers. Just as unbelief is a voluntary concept ("so deeply rooted in our hearts . . . we are so inclined to
it"), so must faith, its opposite, become rooted in the same power
of the soul. As unbelief is "contemptuous of the truth," so faith
is drawn to it and even constitutes obedience to it. The springs
of faith, like those of unbelief, are in the will.

Near the end of his commentary Calvin is still more explicit.
"It will not be enough for the mind to be illumined by the Spirit
of God unless the heart is also strengthened and supported by
his power" (3.2.33). Having said this, Calvin criticizes the Schoolmen who "go completely astray, who in considering faith identify it with a bare and simple assent arising out of knowledge, and
leave out confidence and assurance of heart." Indeed, says Calvin,
"they do not have regard to that firm and steadfast constancy of
heart which is the chief part of faith" (3.2.33). Here Calvin finally
nails down the primacy of the will in faith; he could not be more
definite than when he refers to a "firm and steadfast constancy
of heart which is the chief part of faith." For good measure, consider the neighboring passage, in which he says: "The heart's dis-
trust is greater than the mind's blindness. It is harder for the heart
to be furnished with assurance than for the mind to be endowed
with thought" (3.2.36). At last, then, Calvin secures the voluntarist interpretation of faith that has been implicit since the beginning of 3.2 and thereby brings his concept of faith into harmony
with the voluntaristic description of conversion that precedes his
discussion of faith.[9]

Having established that Calvin has a consistently voluntarist
concept of the will from the fall through the fallen state and into
the redemptive state entered by faith and conversion, I turn now
to an explanation of why, inconsistently with all this, Calvin began
with an intellectualist account of our created state.

Calvin's Method

Why did Calvin fall into an uncritical reliance on Greek intellectualism for his account of intellect and will in our created state? It seems that he failed to adhere to his own stated method, expressed at the beginning of his account, for discovering our nature as it was created, namely, to follow Scripture.

Calvin is quite aware of the question, how can fallen human beings discover anything about the state of perfection that preceded it? The question still is pressed occasionally today.[10] Calvin's answer has two parts: First, we cannot find out what our created nature was like from the pagan philosophers, because they are "ignorant of the corruption of nature that originated from the penalty for man's defection, [and therefore] mistakenly confuse two very diverse states of man" (1.15.7). In their confusion, "they were seeking in a ruin for a building, and in scattered fragments for a well-knit structure" (1.15.8). Their ignorance stemmed, of course, because they lacked the Scripture, which reveals not only the sharp distinction between how we were created in the image of God and our fallen state, but also the way in which we can be restored again through the redemption of Christ.

Hence, the second part of Calvin's answer: that to know the perfection in which we were created we must consult Scripture and, more particularly, the experience of those whose lives have already been changed by the gospel. Says Calvin: The image of God "can be nowhere better recognized than from the restoration of [our] corrupted nature," incomplete as that restoration may be in this life. Scripture also leads believers to contemplate Jesus Christ himself, who is "the most perfect image of God" (1.15.4).

Having expressed his deep doubt that the philosophers can discover the truth about our created state, why does Calvin not stick with Scripture for his account of the created state? The answer, I suggest, is that the Scripture provides only some essential data for a Christian theory of the will and the intellect, not the theory itself. For such a theory, Calvin himself seems to have realized he had to depend, at least in part, on precisely the ancient Greek philosophical tradition he wants to avoid. For we saw him rehearsing not only the medieval conceptions of the will and intellect, but also Plato's and Aristotle's conception of the soul from which the medieval theories were derived.

I have already mentioned Calvin's ambivalence toward philosophy, which extends to the philosophical theology of the Medievals.[11] Couple this ambivalence with his desire to be led first and foremost by Scripture, and one gets a possible explanation for what I have called his first inconsistency, namely, an intellectualist account of our created state that he must abandon immediately for a voluntarist one. At the center of the explanation is Calvin's reluctance to enter into, and work out of, the philosophical-theological tradition that formed him, when he needs to develop his own account of the creation, fall, and redemption of human beings. Had he done so, it seems less likely that he would have fallen into the stark inconsistency we find in his account of the will in its created state. For then he could have taken more explicit account of the voluntarism that originates in Augustine and reaches its definitive formulation in Scotus.

Since philosophers (whether ancient pagan or, we may add, modern secular) have thought deeply about human nature, Christian theologians need a clear idea of how reliable such philosophical accounts can be, offered as they are by thinkers in a fallen state without the advantage of revelation. If pagan and non-Christian philosophers who study human nature are "seeking in a ruin for a building," it is important to ask how much of the "building" is left after the fall for them to see in spite of the ruin, and how much of what is left their own fallen ability and intentions allow them to see.

Not that Calvin has no answer of his own to these questions. In a neighboring passage devoted to the image of God, for example, he says that "some vestige" of the divine image is still present in a fallen human being. Though this image is "not clearly perceived," it can still "arouse him to honor God" (1.15.6). That sounds like a pretty important part of the original building; but the vagueness of the "vestige" metaphor combined with the extensiveness of the ruin as Calvin describes it elsewhere leaves his position on these questions less than fully clear. Still, as we shall see in chapter 5, Calvin has a surprisingly high estimate of the powers of reason after the fall, in contrast to his very low estimate of the human will (which I discuss in chapter 3). Thus there was no need for him to "stick to Scripture alone." In the light of his own account of the rational powers of human beings after the fall, it was entirely consistent for him to turn to the Greek philosophers, and especially to their views as modified by his medieval Christian predecessors, in developing his own account of intellect and will, so long as he also kept Scripture as his guide. It is also understandable why he should have been attracted to Plato more than Aristotle, given the more obviously religious character of Plato's thought. Why he failed to sift his views more carefully, and in particular his intellectualist account of the soul, must be attributed not to his rejection of the inherent worth of their thought but to his own temperamental ambivalence toward engaging it more deeply.

Grace before and after the Fall

Before turning to a remedy for the inconsistency I have discussed in this chapter, I will discuss in passing another topic to which Calvin alludes in the concluding section of his account of the created state (1.15.8), since it raises another dimension of the overall consistency of his teaching about intellect and will. That is the role of divine grace, before and after the fall. Though Calvin does not use the term "grace" in this concluding section, he elsewhere envisages its presence in the created state. For example, he characterizes Adam's fall as lacking gratitude in the pre-fall state "when he abounded with the riches of his grace" (2.2.1). As we will see in more detail later, Calvin accepts Augustine's doctrine that Adam's natural gifts were accompanied by supernatural gifts, which are gifts of grace (2.2.12).

The question of consistency concerns the resistibility of this grace before the fall. Calvin raises the pointed question, why did God create us with a will that is more vulnerable to evil choice than the intellect is to ignorance of good and evil? He concedes to an imagined objector that God could have created us with a nature that "either could not or would not sin at all," and allows that "such a nature would, indeed, have been more excellent."[12] But given that he created the will free, as he did, God could, alternatively, have sustained this will in its freedom "by the virtue of perseverance." Incidentally, since perseverance is a volitional, not an intellectual virtue, what Calvin says here lends further support to the thesis that a voluntarist account of the created state is the only acceptable account. Why God neither created us unable to sin nor sustained the integrity of a nature created capable of sinning, of course, "lies hidden in his plan." Since Adam did fall, however, the grace by which he enjoyed the supernatural gifts must have been resistible.[13] But then that prelapsarian grace before the fall was resistible in a way directly contrary to the irresistible grace that, Calvin teaches, operates on the will in the conversion of human beings from their fallen state and enables them to persevere in the redeemed state (2.3.10,13).

The way out of this inconsistency is suggested by what Calvin says would have happened if Adam had not fallen: "for this exercising of the will would have been followed by perseverance" (1.15.8). He repeats the point in a parallel passage, explicitly attributing such perseverance to grace: "The grace of persisting in good would have been given to Adam if he had so willed" (2.3.13). Thus, the same irresistible grace that believers now enjoy would have been granted in the created state had Adam exercised his will properly, when grace was resistible. The difference is, of course, that in the fallen state only believers receive that irresistible grace and do so in the midst of continuing sins and miseries, whereas if Adam had not fallen all human beings would have persevered in goodness as a result of such grace, and done so in the absence of such sin and misery, even as the redeemed in heaven do now. The consistency is further secured by noting that irresistible grace follows only upon perfect obedience, whether on Adam's part, if he had not sinned, or on Christ's part (the second Adam), who did not sin, and hence on the part of those who share in this feature of Christ's obedience as one aspect of their new life in him.

Be that all as it may, it is clear that Calvin must have a consistently voluntarist conception of the will for the created state. The possibility of sin lies, as Calvin puts it here, in our being created with a "mediocre and even transitory will." Never mind that Calvin here describes the will as "mediocre and transitory," which suggests something less than the highest integrity with which he elsewhere says it was created; that the will is "transitory" suggests only its freedom to sin. The intellect, though it could of course be corrupted by sin, could not be its source. Indeed, the intellect remains strong enough to persist in the knowledge of God in spite of the fall, thereby rendering us without excuse. Far from this strength of intellect implying its primacy over a "weak and transitory will," it is precisely in the will's transitoriness that its power lies to turn us away from the government of the intellect and thereby to undermine its rule. Thus its freedom is the feature of the will that defines its primacy over the intellect.

Hence Calvin's intellectualist account of the will in the created state is simply mistaken. In addition to its being unable to account for the fall, it is also inconsistent with the voluntarist account Calvin gives of the fallen state as well as of conversion from the fallen state, and of faith, conversion's first step, which we now have set forth.

The Remedy

It remains only to point out the remedy required to remove this inconsistency in a Reformed theory of the will. Taking the first step of that remedy is simple enough. It consists in amending the two clearly offending intellectualist passages quoted earlier from Calvin by building into them a primacy of the will. I do this in what follows, paying somewhat more explicit attention than Calvin does to the "minutiae" of Aristotle, Aquinas, and Scotus. The result is a Scotist gloss on Calvin's own language, quoted earlier, which is the view I think he would have taken, had he thought about locating his concept of the will in the medieval tradition that produced him. Here, then, is that first step.

As God created us, the office of reason is to distinguish between ends or objects, whether they are good or evil, as well as between the acts required to attain them, whether they are morally permitted or forbidden; and if they are permitted, how effective they are for the attainment. Reason has no power to move us to act, for that is the function of the will; but the will depends upon the reason as the leader and governor of the soul to propose a course of action to it. In moving us to act, the will by its created nature is inclined to goodness.

65

However, the will is also created with an essential freedom, in virtue of which it can *refuse* to do the first bidding of reason, in favor of pursuing an inferior good the reason might propose. But reason proposes such inferior objects or ends, even perhaps immoral means, only when, in a given situation, the will itself, as it is free and able to do, turns the attention of the intellect *away* from its better knowledge to alternative, "vicious" judgments it is capable of making about ends or means or both. It will do this whenever it is inclined to an inferior good even in the presence of a superior good.

This is the origin of every culpable evil deed. Every such deed consists in an evil choice of the will, which in turn depends on the prior rejection by the will of the intellect's rule, which in turn arises from an evil inclination of the will itself. We are responsible for these deeds, however, because it is by the power of the will that we freely corrupt our intellect as well as choose to act on the corrupted guidance it then gives, without, however, obscuring its better knowledge in the process.

Man in his first condition excelled in these endowments, so that reason and will as they were created not only sufficed for the direction of our earthly life but for seeking all good things from God alone, according to the ordinate inclinations for these good things with which we were created. So Adam could have stood if he wished, seeing that he fell solely by his own will. It was because his will was capable of inclining to lesser goods instead of higher ones, and of corrupting the intellect's judgment by way of these evil inclinations, that he then chose to disobey—in spite of the supernatural gifts with which he was also endowed. This inclination and choice was free, even though the highest rectitude was in both his mind and his will originally, and all the parts of his soul rightly composed to obedience. Why then did Adam choose the evil deed of disobedience? The answer lies in the mystery of the freedom of the created will to turn away from the rule of reason by corrupting it, having first turned away from its own true goodness and integrity.

There it is, an explicitly Scotist Calvin, as I imagine him rewriting his account of the will as God created it in order to avoid his inconsistency. Of course, it is only a brief, programmatic statement, which raises many questions. The answers to these questions require a development of Reformed thought that, as I see it, Reformed philosophers and theologians ought to undertake. As a first step, however, it expresses a consistent, moderately voluntarist view of the will in the Scotist tradition. That is more than any of Calvin's followers, so far as I can tell, have ever done.

The Second Inconsistency: The Fallen Will

We have seen that Calvin gives conflicting accounts of the will as it was created, on the question of its relationship to the intellect. We have also seen which of these accounts, the intellectualist or the voluntarist, must be correct. Calvin has to be a voluntarist; otherwise he cannot explain the role of the will in the fall, in the fallen state, and in the process of conversion, which requires faith as its first step. I turn now to a second conflict in his account of the will, a conflict between his description of the natural components or functions of the will as it was created and his description of these same components or functions in the fallen state.

Like his medieval predecessors, Calvin affirms that the will was created with two main components, inclination and choice. The second inconsistency in Calvin's account of the will is that he denies, for the most part, that the will as so created persists into the fallen state. "For the most part," I say; for as we shall see, of these two components, Calvin retains inclination; but it is no longer an inclination to goodness, only to evil. This reduced concept of the will, I argue, leaves Calvin with a will that is even less than a shadow of its created nature. On Calvin's view, the fall not only corrupts the will, but nearly destroys it. And the result? The result is that Calvin retains in the fallen state so little of the will as it was created that he cannot explain adequately the moral character of human action in that state, when it still makes choices between good and evil.

So his view of the fallen will not only manifests an inconsistency; it is defective as well. In this chapter, I will show both of these points from his *Institutes*, though I will have occasion to refer also to his *Reply to Pighius*.[1] In the next chapter, I offer an explanation of why Calvin falls into his defective account of the fallen will, and in the chapter following that one, I propose an appropriate remedy.

The Augustinian Principle

To bring out the inconsistency in Calvin's thought, it is necessary to note that he has a conviction on whether the created nature of the will persists into the fallen state; it is a conviction that should have headed off his defective account. He shares this conviction with his medieval predecessors, who in turn attribute it to St. Augustine. Hence I shall refer to it as the "Augustinian principle."[2] Calvin first introduces this principle after he is well into a long polemical passage directed against both the philosophers and the medieval theologians (2.2.2–9). It says: "The natural gifts in man were corrupted, but the supernatural taken away" (2.2.4). That Calvin truly espouses this principle is evident from the fact that he repeats it twice when he later sets forth his own account of the fallen intellect and will (2.2.12; 16); then again at the end of a long chapter in which he refutes objections put forward in defense of free will, a chapter which also concludes his entire account of the fall and the fallen state (2.5.19). Thus Calvin literally frames his entire discussion of our fallen state with the Augustinian principle.

His second formulation of the principle is more complete, since it attributes both the corruption of the natural gifts and the loss of the supernatural gifts to sin: "The natural gifts were corrupted in man through sin, but his supernatural gifts were stripped from him" (2.2.12). We must now interpret the distinction the principle draws between the two kinds of gifts, natural and supernatural, in order to expose the inconsistency in Calvin's account of the will. This interpretation, fortunately, will also provide a clue to the appropriate remedy for both the inconsistency and the defect, which I develop later in chapter 5.

The interpretation of the principle hinges on how we should understand what it is in the will (and intellect, which Calvin also has in view) that Calvin refers to with each kind of gift. For merely that each one is a gift does not help, nor that one gift is "natural" and the other "supernatural." In fact, these latter terms are misleading, since both the natural and the supernatural gifts originate in God, who as creator of the natural gifts is no less supernatural with respect to them than he is with respect to the supernatural gifts of his grace. A better hint lies in the statement that one kind of gift is only "corrupted" in us by the fall, whereas the other kind of gift is completely "taken away" or "stripped from us." So something in us was only *corrupted* by the fall; that was our very *nature*. Something else was *taken away* by the fall; that was a *supernatural* gift.

What is this difference between these two kinds of gifts? Calvin himself reveals it when he illustrates each one. First he identifies the supernatural gifts:

> . . . the light of faith as well as righteousness, which would be sufficient to attain heavenly life and eternal bliss. . . . Among these are faith, love of God, charity toward neighbor, zeal for holiness and righteousness. All these, since Christ restores them in us, are considered adventitious, and beyond nature: and for this reason we infer that they were taken away. (2.2.12)

Notice that these gifts (e.g., faith, love of God, zeal for holiness, and the like) are *activities* or *exercises* of the will and intellect, not the natural powers of will or intellect themselves; and they are activities or exercises that depend on divine grace. As gifts of divine grace, they were "sufficient to attain heavenly life" before the fall, even as they are thus sufficient after the fall, when they are restored by grace.[3]

What are the natural gifts? Calvin identifies these as "mind" and "heart" (i.e., intellect and will), which are the natural powers themselves with which we have been created. Though they

71

have lost their *soundness* by having been corrupted, they have not *themselves* been *lost* or *taken away*:

> On the other hand, soundness of mind and uprightness of heart were withdrawn at the same time. This is the corruption of the natural gifts. For even though something of understanding and judgment remains as a residue along with the will, yet we shall not call a mind whole and sound that is both weak and plunged into deep darkness. And depravity of the will is all too well known. (2.2.12)

As gloomy as Calvin's language is with respect to the exercises of the mind (understanding and judgment) and the condition of the will (depravity), it suggests that the powers themselves persist in our fallen state.

Now these powers originate from divine creation, not from divine grace. That is why intellect and will constitute our *nature* as God created it. This nature is, of course, as much a gift as the gifts of grace, but in a way that must be distinguished from them.[4] The distinction is assumed by the familiar formula, "Grace presupposes nature." This formula led to the concept of the special gifts being a *superadditum donum*, which occasioned a dispute between the Reformers and some of the Medievals.[5] Nevertheless, the central thrust of the formula is correct and I hope to show in chapter 5 how it can be maintained in a form acceptable to both sides.

The formula applies to both the created and fallen states. In the created state, divine grace was necessary because of the vulnerability of human nature to sin; in the fallen state, because of the inability of human nature to restore itself to its created state. In either case, the "supernatural" gifts of grace presuppose a nature in which they can be exercised. Otherwise, these gifts would be exercised by no natural powers at all, which would be inconceivable.

The Augustinian principle, thus interpreted, implies that when Calvin comes to describe the components of the will and intellect in their fallen state, he will need to include the very components he attributes to them in their created state—even though neither power is any longer sound and whole, but weakened and corrupted. Accordingly, intellect should retain its natural ability to distinguish between good and evil ends, and between suitable and unsuitable means for attaining these ends. And will should retain, for all its depravity, something of its created inclination to goodness besides its new inclination to evil, as well as its ability to choose between these contrary inclinations. For the idea of corruption, though admittedly vague, does not entail the total loss or destruction of these natural components of the will.[6]

Signs of Departure from the Augustinian Principle

The disappointing fact is, however, that Calvin's actual descriptions of the fallen will (more so than of the intellect) imply not just the corruption, but nearly the complete destruction of its natural components. An early sign of this betrayal of the Augustinian principle with respect to the will appears already in the second passage quoted above from 2.2.12, in which Calvin interprets the principle as distinguishing a natural power in us (with its corresponding natural exercises) from supernatural exercises of that power (which are dependent on grace). Recall that this passage, while allowing some understanding and judgment to the fallen intellect, ascribes nothing but *depravity* to the fallen will.

Calvin continues this markedly different treatment of the intellect and the will in his initial application of the principle. This initial application (also found in 2.2.12) provides a good summary of the lengthy elaboration of the fallen intellect and will that follows it (2.2.12–27). It is, therefore, worth quoting in full:

> Since reason, therefore, by which man distinguishes between good and evil, and by which he understands and judges, is a natural gift, it could not be completely wiped out; but it was partly weakened and partly corrupted, so that its misshapen ruins appear. John speaks in this sense: "The light still shines in the darkness, but the darkness comprehends it not" [John 1:5]. In these words both facts are expressed. First, in man's perverted and degenerate nature some sparks still gleam. These show him to be a rational being, differing from brute beasts, because he is endowed with understanding. Yet, secondly, they show this light choked with dense ignorance, so that it cannot come forth effectively.

> Similarly the will, because it is inseparable from man's nature, did not perish, but was so bound to wicked desires that it cannot strive for what is right. This is, indeed, a complete definition, but one needing fuller explanation. (2.2.12)

Notice that Calvin distinguishes with some care the natural functions of the intellect that survive the fall from the corruption that plagues them. By contrast (not "similarly," as he claims), he offers nearly nothing to distinguish the natural functions of the will (inclination to goodness and moral choice) as they survive from the corruption that plagues them. "Nearly nothing," I say, for inclination survives; but it is "so bound to wicked desires that it cannot strive for what is right." In other words, the will's created inclination for goodness has been wholly lost; it has been simply replaced by an inclination to evil. Such a loss, of course, will rule out the survival of any ability to choose between good and evil, let alone to "strive for what is right."

Two more signs of Calvin's departure from the Augustinian principle with respect to the will are even more conspicuous: his titles for chapters 2 and 3. The title of the former, which contains the heart of his discussion of the fallen will is: "Man Has Now Been Deprived of Freedom of Choice and Bound over to Miserable Servitude." Deprived of free choice? With no difference between a corrupted choice and no choice at all? As we shall see, that is just what Calvin believes and defends. Miserable servitude? With no qualification to accommodate the Augustinian distinction between corruption and destruction? So we shall soon see. His title for chapter 3 is no more encouraging: "Only Damnable Things Come Forth from Man's Corrupt Nature." Corrupted goodness turns out to be not *corrupted* goodness (goodness corrupted by evil), but *no* goodness at all.

The Bondage of the Will

Let us now see how all this works out in Calvin's discussion, both of the will's created inclination for goodness and for its created power of choice. First, however, two preliminary comments are in order, one logistical, the other substantial; but they are interrelated. Logistically, it turns out that, although Calvin outlines his important chapter 2 to discuss the fallen will in sections 26–27, after the fallen intellect in 12–25, those two sections deal all too briefly with it. Hence we shall have to consider also an earlier passage (2.2.2–8), which is a polemic against the philosophers and the fathers. The substantial issue is the *bondage of the will*, a theme that pervades these discussions. The theme reveals how Calvin conceives the effect of the fall on the relationship between inclination and choice, with respect to conversion; but more than this, by failing to distinguish carefully between this latter point and the fallen will in itself, Calvin's discussion conveys much of his view of the fallen will itself, considered apart from conversion.

Near the end of the two sections just referred to (2.2.26–27), Calvin formulates the doctrine of the bondage of the will, having just cited John 8:34 ("Everyone who commits sin is a slave to sin"):

> We are all sinners by nature; therefore we are held under the yoke of sin. But if the whole man lies under the power of sin, surely it is necessary that the will, which is its chief seat, be restrained by the stoutest bonds. (2.2.27)

I quoted this passage in chapter 2 to underscore Calvin's voluntarist account of sin, with its reference to the will as "its chief seat." Before showing the significance of this passage for the present issue, whether the will is the source of nothing but evil, we need to identify three important points it raises.

First, we must clarify the phrase that we are "sinners by nature." Earlier Calvin has taken pains to note the ambiguity of the phrase "by nature":

> Therefore we declare that man is corrupted through natural vitiation, but a vitiation that did not flow from nature. We deny that it has flowed from nature in order to indicate that it is an adventitious quality which comes upon man rather than a substantial property which has been implanted from the beginning. (2.1.11)

So Calvin's meaning is that we are sinners not by our nature, strictly speaking (i.e., as created), but by our *corrupted* nature (i.e., by a corruption that is not original in our nature as created).

In other words, our nature as created gives us a "substantial property," but as corrupted, an "adventitious quality." Calvin invokes an Aristotelian distinction to pick out the defining properties that constitute human beings as human from their sinfulness, which does not. He thereby reiterates a point, following Augustine and the medieval theologians, against the Manichean heresy, on which human nature is essentially both good and evil, reflecting an ultimate dualism of good and evil in the universe.[7]

Second, the phrase about the "whole man" lying under the power of sin is likewise ambiguous. Does it mean that evil corrupts every aspect of human activity or that human beings are nothing but evil in these aspects? The resolution of this ambiguity is much less clear. Calvin moves all too easily from the first sense to the second: "We are so vitiated and perverted in every part of our nature that we stand justly condemned and convicted before God. . . . Indeed, their whole nature [i.e., of the infants who transmit original sin] is a seed of sin; hence it can be only hateful and abhorrent to God" (2.1.8). Can Calvin really mean to teach here that God sees nothing left in the fallen state of the nature he himself created that is good and pleasing? Again, Calvin writes: "Whatever is in man, from the understanding to the will, from the soul even to the flesh, has been defiled and crammed with this concupiscence. Or, to put it more briefly, the whole man is of himself nothing but conscupiscence" (2.1.8). Notice that each quotation ends by suggesting that evil is the *only* power at work in fallen human nature.[8]

Third, to what does the phrase "restrained by the stoutest bonds" refer? Calvin here certainly refers to the power of sin, but does sin so stoutly bind the will in every possible aspect of its inclination and choice, or only those pertaining to its conversion back to God? That is the central question inevitably raised by Calvin's doctrine of the bondage of the will. Let us now look more closely at his detailed elaborations, focusing upon each component of the will in turn.

The Inclination of the Will Wholly Evil

Calvin is well aware of the pagan Greek philosophical tradition that "all things seek good through a natural instinct, and that this view is received with general consent" (2.2.26). It would seem that he might credit this tradition with an insight, reached apart from revelation, into the goodness of the universe as it came forth from the hand of God, but things go quite differently. In order to head off the will's power to choose good over evil as a special case of this "natural instinct" in human beings, Calvin proceeds directly to eliminate the instinct for goodness from the will, at least with respect to any moral inclination to goodness that would count as an essential component in human happiness:

> But that we may not suppose this [philosophical] doctrine to have anything to do with the uprightness of the human will, let us observe that the power of free choice is not to be sought in such an appetite, which arises from inclination of nature rather than from deliberation of mind. (2.2.26)

Here Calvin makes the valid point that choice between good and evil presupposes their presentation to the will by the mind. What is dubious is that he cuts off the will's choice between moral good and evil from any prior *natural* inclination to goodness in the will itself, which it might retain as a restraint on the evil inclinations that now also characterize its fallen state. Clearly, if the will's prior instinct or inclination is morally evil without any qualification, there can be no motive left in the will for choosing a morally good alternative instead of an evil one; every choice is doomed from the start to be a choice of evil.

That is just what Calvin's continued description suggests:

> And actually, if you consider the character of this natural desire of good in man, you will find that he has it in common with animals. For they also desire their own well-being; and when some sort of good that can move their sense appears, they follow it. But man does not choose by reason and pursue with zeal what is truly good for himself according to the excellence of his immortal nature; nor does he use his reason in deliberation or bend his mind to it. Rather, like an animal, he follows the inclination of his nature, without reason, without deliberation. Therefore whether or not man is impelled to seek after good by an impulse of nature has no bearing upon the freedom of the will. This instead is required: that he discern good by right reason; that knowing it he choose it; that having chosen it he follow it.[9] (2.2.26)

Not only does Calvin here deny any sense of moral goodness in the fallen state, he does so by almost completely denying that there is even any desire in the will for distinctively human happiness. Calvin is willing enough to admit we retain a desire for happiness, but he proceeds immediately to diminish the human quality of this desire by asserting that in our fallen state this desire is no different from that of the animals (even "without reason, without deliberation"). Thus his claim, in effect, is that the human will in its fallen state is bereft of any rational, distinctively human desire, either for happiness or for any aspect of the moral goodness and virtue essential to that happiness.[10]

In the next section (2.2.27) Calvin elaborates his answer to the question he asks at the end of section 26: "whether in other respects the will is so deeply vitiated and corrupted in its every part that it can beget nothing but evil; or whether it retains any portion unimpaired, from which good desires may be born." His elaboration will affirm the former alternative, that indeed the fallen will has lost all its inclination to moral goodness and deny the latter, that the fallen will retains any "portion unimpaired, from which good desires may be born."

The elaboration is oriented to the struggle between good and evil described by Paul in Romans 7. Calvin interprets Paul to refer exclusively to a struggle in Christian experience, between the new desires for the "supernatural gifts" kindled by regenerating grace and the old, evil desires of the fallen will.[11] The possibility of doing no evil ("I myself do not do evil, but sin that dwells in me"), says Calvin, "applies only to the regenerate who tend toward good with the chief part of their soul"; apart from such regeneration, in other words, the fallen natural will retains no inclination to moral goodness at all.

This analysis of Romans 7 leads Calvin to assert the bondage of the will in the passage quoted earlier, when I mentioned the importance of that idea in Calvin's discussion of the fallen will. I referred there to some important points raised by his formulation of that doctrine: one regarding the ambiguity of the phrase "the corruption of the whole man"; another, the question of what Calvin refers to when he asserts that this corruption needs to be "restrained by the stoutest bonds." It seems in order now to observe that Calvin's analysis of Romans 7 suggests that there is no moral power at all left in the *nature* of the fallen will, and that consequently the only available restraint for its evil desires is from beyond its nature, in the form of the regenerating grace of the Holy Spirit.

Calvin concludes the section (and chapter 2 as a whole) on a polemical note: "Away then with all that 'preparation' which many [Catholic theologians] babble about." It is clear that Calvin here wants to head off the semi-Pelagian view that the fallen will, apart from saving grace, can take a first step (involving, no doubt, both inclination and choice) toward faith. We need to return to this polemical remark, and others like it, to see how it may have affected Calvin's analysis of the fallen will. For now, it seems clear that, having affirmed the wholly evil inclination of the will, Calvin has sealed the fate of free choice between good and evil in the fallen state. For how could a wholly evil inclination dispose a will to choose any good whatsoever over evil?

The Free Choice of the Will between Good and Evil

Calvin's vigorous denial of the will's free choice is well known. As Lane observes, "A slender volume could be produced comprised [sic] solely of Calvin's attacks on free will."[12] Calvin does not elaborate this attack in the two brief sections (26–27) that have occupied our attention so far, in which he purports to set forth his account of the will in the fallen state. As indicated earlier, he has already done this in sections 2–11, where he argues against both the Greek philosophers and the Church Fathers. Let us take a brief look at this polemic.

Calvin is just as aware of the testimony of the ancient pagan philosophers to free choice between good and evil as he is of that same testimony to the will's basic inclination to goodness.

> They say: If to do this or that depends upon our choice, so also does not to do it. Again, if not to do it, so also to do it. Now we seem to do what we do, and to shun what we shun, by free choice. Therefore, if we do any good thing when we please, we can also not do it; if we do any evil, we can also shun it. (2.2.3)

Calvin goes on to criticize the philosophers for their failure to see moral virtue, which is acquired by freely choosing morally right acts, as a gift of God and to thank God for it. That failure, to praise God for moral goodness, is owing to their fallen state, of course; but it is also a different issue, as I shall show later (in chapter 4), when I explain what motivates Calvin to argue so vigorously against free choice.

The ancient philosophical view that virtue and vice are developed by performing actions freely chosen has as its corollary that virtue and vice are not gifts of fortune like beauty or noble birth. As inner states of character, they are "within our power"; that is why we are responsible for them: "The Greeks were not ashamed to use a much more presumptuous word [than 'free will']. They called it 'self-power,' as if each man had power in his own hands" (2.2.4). What Calvin objects to here is an attitude of independence (presumptuousness) occasioned by the concept, not to the concept itself.[13] But his concern about this attitude leads him to miss the point of the concept, which is to distinguish our rational-moral nature from that of the animals. Our moral character, which animals lack, is developed by our own actions, which, in turn, depend upon our own choices, which, in turn, are a function of our intellect and will.

Having discussed the ancient philosophers, Calvin proceeds to discuss the use made of their teachings by the Church Fathers and the medieval theologians. He cites Origen as typical of the Fathers, who spoke of free choice as "a faculty of the reason to distinguish between good and evil, a faculty of the will to choose one or the other"; and Aquinas as typical of the theologians, who spoke of free choice as "a 'power of selection' which, derived from a mingling of understanding and appetite, yet inclines more to appetite" (2.2.4). He concludes his summary of the Fathers and Schoolmen, however, with the warning: "It remains for us to see briefly how much they attribute to each [reason and will]."

Too much, Calvin thinks, in the way of moral goodness apart from grace. His own position is "that free will is not sufficient to enable man to do good works, unless he be helped by grace, indeed, by special grace, which only the elect receive through regeneration" (2.2.6). He will demonstrate "whether man has been wholly deprived of all power to do good, or still has some power, though meager and weak; a power, indeed, that can do nothing of itself, but with the help of grace also does its part."

Calvin opposes Lombard, who "hints that man by his very own nature somehow seeks after the good," and others who suggest that by our nature we can even "confirm [the work of divine grace] by obediently following it" (2.2.6). But in opposing Lombard's hint, in the interest of defending the necessity of grace for salvation and the good works peculiar to it, Calvin fails to qualify either the crucial phrase "wholly deprived of the power to do good" or his denial that fallen man "by his very own nature somehow seeks after the good." Thus it is easy to conclude that Calvin denies for the fallen state any freedom of choice between good and evil, any power to do any good at all.

A Soteriological Defense

It may be objected at this point that the above analysis of Calvin's view of the fallen will ignores his overriding concern, which is to expose the semi-Pelagian account of conversion in some of the medieval theologians. Much can be conceded to this objection, which I will call the soteriological defense. No doubt it explains some of the oversimplification in Calvin's exposition. Still, oversimplification is what it is. Says Calvin: "God so commends his grace to us that we know that we are nothing. By God's mercy alone we stand, since by ourselves we are nothing but evil" (2.2.11). One can allow Calvin such rhetorical excess to make his point against the semi-Pelagians that there is no power in the fallen will to turn back to God apart from grace; that in this respect the fallen will is simply evil. In a similar way, the defense can explain the prevalence of Calvin's polemic against the semi-Pelagians, which tends to dominate his entire exposition of the fallen will.

As part of this defense, it may also be objected that I have failed to notice those passages in which Calvin refers, either implicitly or explicitly, to the fallen will in itself, in spite of his overriding soteriological interest. For example, in a passage cited earlier, Calvin refers to the "truly good": "But man does not choose by reason and pursue with zeal what is truly good for himself according to the excellence of his immortal nature" (2.2.26). It could be argued that Calvin's reference here to what is truly good implies the possibility in the fallen will for something less than truly good. My answer to this argument is that Calvin should then have developed this distinction and thereby aligned himself with classical philosophers and Christian theologians before him who do just that. They commonly distinguish what is *good* in and for human beings from what is their *highest good*. But Calvin does not do this; he typically blurs the line between these two concepts and suggests that the highest good is the only good there is, so that when that goodness is lost in the fall, no other moral good is left.

It can be granted, further, that Calvin explicitly acknowledges the distinction the Schoolmen draw between "earthly" and "heavenly" things: "Under man's free counsel they commonly class those intermediate things which obviously do not pertain to God's Kingdom; but they refer true righteousness to God's special grace and spiritual regeneration" (2.2.5). And again:

> When the church fathers are discussing free will, they first inquire, not into its importance for civil or external actions, but into what promotes obedience to the divine law. Although I grant this latter question is the main one, I do not think the former ought to be completely neglected. I hope I shall render a very good account of my own opinion. (2.2.5)

So Calvin openly acknowledges that an account of the fallen will for "earthly things" apart from saving grace is required; he even expresses his "hope to render a very good account" of it. I have argued, however, that in the passages so far discussed Calvin fails to do this with respect to the surviving goodness of the will and its power of moral choice.

He does presently begin such an account (in 2.3.3–4), just before he directly addresses the topic of conversion (in 2.3.6–14). There he writes: "In every age there have been persons who, guided by nature, have striven toward virtue throughout life" (2.3.3). I will examine these sections later, in chapter 5, as the background for proposing my own remedy to his account. There I will show what is missing in Calvin's account, insofar as he intends to explain the goodness of people in the fallen state.

My main response to the soteriological defense is that, although it can explain some of the shortcomings in Calvin's account of the fallen will, it does not justify them. Calvin's descriptions of the fallen state from which grace rescues us typically and pervasively claim or assume its unqualifiedly evil character. For example, commenting on St. Paul, Calvin observes that Paul's intention "is not simply to rebuke men that they may repent, but rather to teach them that they have all been overwhelmed by an unavoidable calamity from which only God's mercy can deliver them" (2.3.2). So far so good: the fallen state, for all the natural gifts that persist in it, *is* a calamity not only because these natural gifts (read: *powers*) are corrupted, but especially because the supernatural gifts (read: *special exercises* of faith, hope, and love) on which the healing of these powers depends have been altogether lost. But note what Calvin says next: "Because this [calamity] could not be proved unless it rested upon the ruin and *destruction of our nature*, he [Paul] put forward these testimonies which prove our *nature* utterly lost." And again, "it is futile to seek anything good in our *nature*. . . . The soul, plunged into this deadly abyss, is not only burdened with vices but is *utterly devoid* of all good" (2.3.2; emphases mine).

Calvin here goes quite beyond what is required to make his soteriological point. His quotations from Paul do not imply "the destruction of nature," nor, as we shall see later, does Calvin himself on other occasions seem to find it "futile to seek anything good in our nature." Thus his unqualified conclusion here, that "the soul is utterly devoid of all good" is just false. To be sure, every time we read such extreme pronouncements, we could say to ourselves: "Of course, Calvin means here 'only with respect to conversion.'"[14] But is Calvin entitled to such generosity on the part of his reader? Not if, after all, the topic he has set for himself in these chapters is not conversion but the nature of the fallen will *in itself*. Notice that the chapter title of Book 2 that first refers to conversion is that of chapter 4: "How God Works in Men's Hearts." The titles of all the preceding three chapters refer to the fall and its consequences, supposedly considered in themselves apart from the special work of God required for conversion.

So one could wish that Calvin had given a sustained account of the nature of the fallen will as such, without running ahead of himself in these three chapters by slipping so frequently into a polemic against mistaken views of conversion. But that is just what he fails to do. Says Calvin, "Because of the bondage of sin by which the will is held bound, it cannot move toward good, much less apply itself thereto; for a movement of this sort is the beginning of conversion to God, which in Scripture is ascribed entirely to God's grace" (2.3.5). Notice that he just fails to *qualify* the phrase "cannot move toward good" to distinguish the good toward which the fallen will might still move by its very created nature from the supernatural good that is the beginning of the will's conversion to God.

Again, he implies the total loss of the will's inclination to goodness, while saying nevertheless that the natural will remains: "Nonetheless the will remains, with the most eager inclination disposed and hastening to sin. For man, when he gave himself over to this necessity, was not deprived of will, but of soundness of will" (2.3.5). In other words, either the will is sound (as it was in creation and can become again after conversion) or it is nothing but eagerly disposed to sin. Calvin simply ignores a third alternative, required by the Augustinian principle, that something of the will's own created inclination to goodness might persist into the fallen state, *without* being wholly lost in the way that the supernatural gifts were lost.

It is surprising that Calvin should think he has to eliminate all inclination to goodness in the will for, like every Christian theologian, he has the best theological reason for retaining something of it in the fallen will. This is the doctrine of creation, which entails the goodness of human nature as it comes from the hand of God. Yet consider what he writes: "Surely there is ready and sufficient reason to believe that good takes its origin from God alone. And only in the elect does one find a will inclined to good" (2.3.8). He continues, commenting on Ezekiel 11:19:

> He [God] testifies that our conversion is the creation of a new spirit and a new heart. What other fact could more clearly claim for him, and take away from us, every vestige of good and right in our will? For it always follows that nothing good can arise out of our will until it has been reformed; after its reformation, in so far as it is good, it is so from God. (2.3.8)

But it does not follow from God's "creating a new spirit and heart" by grace in the fallen will that such regeneration must "take away from us every vestige of good and right in our will." Indeed,

Calvin could have allowed much more than just a vestige of the will's goodness to survive in the fall, so long as it excluded the possibility of a first step toward conversion. As I shall argue, this survival of a created goodness in the fallen will is what the Augustinian principle, properly understood, requires.

So the question is, why does Calvin repeatedly write as if God must show his grace at the cost of the very nature of the will as he created it?[15] It is no wonder, in light of such passages, that Calvin's Catholic critics complain that he disparages nature to magnify grace. If both nature and grace are from God, there is no need to fear giving nature its full due in its fallen state. Calvin's rightful objection to a semi-Pelagian account of conversion gives him no leave to minimize the structure of the natural will and its natural inclination to goodness as these both persist into the fallen state. I shall pursue these points when I propose an appropriate remedy to Calvin's unqualified rejection of the fallen will's inclination to goodness and its power to choose good over evil. For now, it is sufficient to point out that the soteriological defense of Calvin's account of the fallen will against my analysis of it is inadequate. The need for a soteriologically correct account of the role of grace in salvation does not excuse Calvin (or his Reformed followers) for a defective account of the volitional effects of the fall.

The Minimalist Defense

I turn now to a second possible objection to my account. It might be said that Calvin does not need the will's inclination to goodness or its power of contrary choice between good and evil in its fallen state to maintain its responsibility for its bondage to sin. I will call this response the minimalist defense of Calvin's view of the fallen will. On this defense, the inconsistency I point out between Calvin's view of the will as it was created and as it persists into the fallen state will not matter, since Calvin can still maintain its full responsibility for its fallen condition. The defense assumes, of course, that maintaining such responsibility is all that matters. The assumption is false, as I will show in the section that follows.

That Calvin really does want to maintain this minimalist view is evident from a reference to the "sounder Schoolmen," who he thinks agree with him. As an example, he again cites Lombard (whose hint at some natural goodness in the will he has just rejected):

> For Lombard finally declares that we have free will, not in that we are equally capable of doing or thinking good and evil, but merely that we are freed from compulsion. According to Lombard, this freedom is not hindered, even if we be wicked and slaves of sin, and can do nothing but sin. (2.2.6)

Note that Calvin here distinguishes *freedom from compulsion* from *freedom of choice* (being "equally capable of doing or thinking good and evil"), which he rejects (as we have already seen). This freedom from compulsion is the freedom of the will to follow its own inclination in the choices it makes. Of this freedom Calvin says, "it so inheres in man by nature that it cannot possibly be taken away" (2.2.6). Interestingly, this freedom from compulsion can be compared to the freedom of spontaneity that we examined in chapter 1, as just another way of defining what I there called the minimalist concept of free will. Hence Calvin's doctrine of the bondage of the will can be understood consistently either with the will's spontaneous pursuit of evil or with its pursuit of evil free from any external compulsion or necessity. And, according to the minimalist defense, this understanding of the fallen will is sufficient to maintain its responsibility for the evil it commits.[16]

Before exploring the significance of this claim, I will digress for a moment, which is just what Calvin also does. Having insisted on this freedom from compulsion as essential to the nature of the will, he suddenly asks: ". . . but what purpose is served by labeling with a proud name such a slight thing? A noble freedom, indeed—for man not to be forced to serve sin, yet to be such a willing slave that his will is bound by the fetters of sin!" (2.2.7). The context suggests that Calvin means here to contrast the bondage of sin (which presupposes this freedom from compulsion nevertheless) with the highest freedom, namely, freedom *from* such bondage to sin, which grace makes possible in conversion. As important as this contrast is, making it here, as Calvin does, diminishes the significance that Calvin must ascribe to this minimalist sense of freedom for maintaining the responsibility of the will for the bondage of sin. Since he must do the latter, and has invoked the minimalist sense of free will for this purpose, why would he suddenly scorn this sense?

Actually, since he needs to insist upon it, let us get back on that track, in order to see whether it is sufficient for him to maintain the will's responsibility for its sorry state. Expositing Augustine, he writes:

> When the will was conquered by the vice into which it had fallen, human nature began to lose its freedom. Again, man, using free will badly, has lost both himself and his will. Again, the free will has been so enslaved that it can have no power for righteousness. (2.2.7)

Notice that the will is "conquered by vice," but a vice "into which it had fallen." Calvin's point is that the bondage of vice is not original in the will; the will has "fallen" into it. That is, the bondage of vice is one thing, how it is acquired, another. It was acquired, Calvin says, by "using free will badly." This phrase must refer to the prelapsarian will. That will, of course, consisted not only of an inclination to goodness but also the power to choose between good and evil. Having chosen disobedience, "man . . . has lost both himself and his will." Does Calvin mean that we lost our will entirely? or just choice? We have already seen his explicit answer: not only choice but even the original inclination to moral goodness.

Similarly, expositing Bernard later on, Calvin observes: "We are oppressed by no other yoke than that of a kind of voluntary servitude" (2.3.5). "Voluntary" here refers ambiguously either to the servitude by which we willingly *remain* in our fallen state or to the willing way in which we *entered* that servitude. The latter willingness, however, entails the freedom of choice that was an essential component of the created nature, which made the primal act of disobedience possible; but the former does not. And now we can ask two questions: is the fact that we entered the bondage of the will by a free choice sufficient for maintaining reponsibility for the continued evildoing in which that bondage

consists? And can one lose an original power of choice for goodness and still be responsible for the evildoing one commits?

Aristotle long ago suggested that the answer to both questions
is yes. In his account of how we acquire virtues and vices, he
writes:

> Our actions and our characteristics [i.e. our habits, and by exten-
> sion, our characters] are not voluntary in the same sense: we are
> in control of our actions from beginning to end, insofar as we
> know the particular circumstances surrounding them. But we
> control only the beginning of our characteristics: the particular
> steps in their development are imperceptible, just as they are in
> the spread of disease; yet since the power to behave or not to
> behave in a given way was ours in first place, our characteristics
> are voluntary.[17]

So if the bondage of sin is like a vice, our continued responsibility for the evil we do in this state of bondage can arise in the same
way as it does in a vice, namely, by the wrong choice that preceded it, which can no longer be undone. But then the inconsistency between Calvin's maximalist account of the created will
and his minimalist account of the fallen will does not matter,
which is the point of the minimalist defense. The defense is still
limited, however, to the issue of retaining responsibility for the
actions of the fallen will. The question is, does this make it a sufficient defense of Calvin's position? The answer is no, since more
is at stake in Calvin's minimalist position on the fallen will than
the issue of maintaining our responsibility, as we shall now see.[18]

The Consequences of Calvin's Minimalist View of the Fallen Will

There must be other reasons than mere inconsistency, then,
for holding Calvin to the Augustinian principle. There are, and
they are independent of the fact that Calvin himself affirms that
principle. That he affirms the principle makes his categorical
denials of the fallen will's inclination to goodness and its power
of contrary moral choice inconsistent with his description of the
created will. That his minimalist view of the fallen will, on which
its only defining feature is an exclusive inclination to evil, is defec-

tive can be argued independently of this inconsistency. I do this now by indicating four significant consequences that follow from it. These consequences provide a cumulative case that shows not only why Calvin's minimalist account of the freedom of the fallen will must be mistaken, but also why a (qualified[19]) maximalist account of the fallen will is necessary.

First, Calvin's minimalist view has the consequence that by the misuse of the will in the fall human beings were able nearly to destroy the very nature and structure with which it was originally created by God. For on Calvin's view, the fallen will is but a shadow of its former self, without its power to choose between good and evil and without any of its original inclination to goodness. But how could the will, in an evil choice that deprived it of its supernatural gifts, also destroy its very own *nature* to such a great extent? Only, it would appear, by a voluntarism far more radical than Calvin needs, in order to account adequately for the fallen state, a voluntarism so radical that the will has power not only to do wrong, and thereby corrupt itself, but also nearly to destroy its very own essence.

To see how radical such a consequence is, put it this way: God so created the human will that it could through disobedience destroy itself almost beyond recognition as the human faculty God himself created it to be. But is it really likely that God created the human will with that much power? That he created the will able to fall is evident, even if pretty mysterious (as we noted in chapter 1); but that he created it nearly able to wipe out of existence its own nature verges on the incredible. Nor does Calvin anywhere (that I know) explain why so total a loss of the inclination for goodness and contrary choice between good and evil is required to preserve the necessity of saving grace for the restoration of the supernatural gifts that were lost. I will suggest in the next chapter, however, what may have led him to this view, mistakenly and without his knowing it.

The second consequence of Calvin's minimalist view, that every desire of the fallen will is evil so that it is quite unable to choose any good, is to render unintelligible the moral choices between good and evil that human beings continue to make in their fallen state. Of course, Calvin still recognizes the possibility and actuality of such choices in the fallen state (albeit in a way that is sometimes less than fully clear). My point is that he cannot *account for* such choices, since they arise from a will that has lost its inclination for goodness as well as its power to choose between good and evil. Given the exclusively evil motivation of the will, it can make only an evil choice in the face of every alternative between good and evil proposed to it by the intellect. But then the knowledge of good and evil that the intellect still retains in the fallen state, which Calvin acknowledges, is pointless for offering moral guidance to the fallen will.[20]

Third, and flowing directly from this second consequence, the choice between good and evil, whenever it is presented to the will by reason, can never even be *felt* in the fallen state as a moral conflict between good and evil; for such a conflict presupposes the presence of opposite inclinations between good and evil, not just an intellectual formulation of the alternatives. This implication of Calvin's account of the fallen will, however, is contrary to all human experience in the fallen state, experience that is abundantly attested to in the history and literature of the world. To be sure, Calvin refers at one point to Medea's conflict and to Aristotle's analysis of incontinence (2.2.7). But on his account of the fallen will, as I have detailed it so far, the entire human history of moral conflict between good and evil, let alone its vivid portrayal in literature and studious examination by pagan philosophers, is a chimera. The only genuine conflict between good and evil is the conflict experienced by Christian believers, as we saw earlier in his interpretation of Romans 7.

A fourth consequence follows from the third. If fallen human beings cannot feel the struggle between good and evil in their lives, there will be no analogy in their fallen experience by which they can even understand the gospel itself. For the gospel poses the special (indeed, ultimate) conflict that fallen human beings need to feel between the evil of their having rejected (and thereby lost) the supernatural gifts of trusting and loving God and enjoying his favor, and the good of their possessing these supernatural gifts once again through faith in the gospel. Now a theory of the fallen will that remedies this defect, such as I have hinted at and will propose later, does not need to imply any meritorious contribution of the fallen reason or will toward the beginning of this faith. On this critical point, Calvin can still insist that the beginning of faith, true righteousness, and genuine happiness are dependent on saving grace. A corrected account of the fallen will, however, will head off the suggestion of Calvin's account that divine grace operates in a total vacuum by creating an entirely new will that has little, if any, continuity with the natural will as it was originally created, a new will that seems rather artificially juxtaposed to the minimal structure of the fallen will that, on Calvin's description of it, is nothing but a spontaneous pursuit of evil.

I conclude from these unhappy consequences of Calvin's minimalist view of the fallen will that the view is mistaken and also that a corrected account will have to involve a (qualified) maximalist view of it. Before proposing that corrected account, I want to show, in chapter 4, what seems to have led Calvin to his mistaken view.

Pride after the Fall

What led Calvin into so defective an account of the fallen will? Loose ends in Calvin's thought have often been attributed variously to his rhetorical style, his disapproval of "speculation," or his ambivalence toward philosophy. These explanations doubtless contain some truth, but there is a much more specific explanation for Calvin's rather wholesale denial of free will and moral goodness in our fallen state. That explanation lies in his preoccupation with the danger of human pride.

Calvin's Warning against Pride

A persistent warning against pride permeates Calvin's writings and has been widely noted. Leith observes that Calvin's warning is relevant even to understanding his doctrine of the will:

> Calvin's discussion of the will cannot be understood apart from three peculiar qualities of his theology which contributed to the intelligibility of faith in his particular cultural and religious situation, namely (1) the doxological character of his theology which seeks to give God the glory, which focuses attention on the immediacy of the divine lordship and grace and minimizes the

orders and structures and energies of human action, (2) his great fear of a false and dangerous confidence in works, and (3) the modesty and awe that is the proper human stance in the presence of the majesty and hiddeness of God.[1]

Leith claims rightly that these themes are pervasive in Calvin. Rather than contributing to the "intelligibility" of Calvin's account of the will, however, I will argue that these themes (especially the first two) are just what lead Calvin to an *un*intelligible view of the will, the mistaken view I have described. If my argument is correct, Calvin's view should have been found equally unintelligible in his own "cultural and religious situation." As a matter of fact, it was found unintelligible by Albert Pighius and Desiderius Erasmus, to mention just two prominent names.

Calvin's warning against pride already contributes to the tone of the opening chapters of the *Institutes,* where he sets forth his two well-known ingredients of "true and sound wisdom," namely, "the knowledge of God and of ourselves" (1.1.1). The essence of this twofold knowledge is that human beings owe every good thing they enjoy, both in their creation and their redemption, to God alone. "The mighty gifts with which we are endowed are hardly from ourselves; indeed, our very being is nothing but subsistence in the one God." The proper response that accompanies such knowledge is piety, humility, and gratitude (1.1.1; 1.2.1). Hence, our first and ultimate sin is pride and self-assurance, our failure to acknowledge our complete dependence upon God for every good gift by crediting whatever good thing we enjoy to our own account (1.2.2; 1.4.2).

Calvin reviews the theme of pride at the beginning of the first chapter of Book 2, before giving an account of the fall, and then again in the second chapter, before turning to the effects of the fall on the will and intellect. He warns against a perverse application of the Delphic oracle "Know yourself!" in the following comment: "This, we observe, has happened to certain philosophers, who, while urging man to know himself, propose the goal of recognizing his own worth and excellence. And they would have him contemplate in himself nothing but what swells him with empty assurance and puffs him up with pride" (2.1.1).

Calvin's warning against pride reflects the biblical teaching that pride is the original sin. The question then is, how did so laudable a concern result in so defective an account of the will? The answer, in short, is Calvin's mistaken assumption that the only way to avoid human pride is to *deny* human goodness and free will. In what follows, I will show that this is his assumption and that it must be mistaken.

Having described the fall in Book 2, chapter 1, Calvin begins chapter 2 with a statement of the "bondage of the will," one of the main results of the fall. Then he introduces the central topic of the chapter, which is "to investigate more closely whether we have been deprived of all freedom since we have been reduced to this servitude; and, if any particle of it still survives, how far its power extends" (2.2.1). He continues: "In order that the truth of this question may be more readily apparent to us, I shall presently set a goal to which the whole argument should be directed" (2.2.1). We have already seen (and will presently see again) just what Calvin believes is the truth about the will's bondage, namely, that it has no free choice between good and evil, and that the only "particle" of freedom that survives the fall is the spontaneous pursuit of evil.

But what is the "goal to which the whole argument should be directed"? That goal is nothing less than to warn against the human pride, self-assurance, and ingratitude that characterizes the fallen state; or, more positively, to inspire his readers in humility to give God alone the glory and praise for all the goodness in our lives. We shall see, however, that Calvin confuses that laudable, pastoral goal with the double question at hand, namely, how much free will and how much moral goodness (both gifts of our created nature) persist beyond the fall into the fallen state? In fact, Calvin *links* the two together: the goal of avoiding pride requires the denial of freedom and moral goodness in the fallen state. This linkage is evident both in the introductory section of chapter 2, just cited, and in two later sections (10 and 11), which precede his eventual exposition of the noetic (12–25) and volitional (26–27) effects of the fall. Let us examine his argument in both of these places.

Answering a Dilemma

Calvin's opening argument takes the form of his answer to a dilemma, a dilemma derived (as he notes) from Augustine. Here is the dilemma in its simplest form: either we *can't* be good, in which case we *won't try* to be good or we *can* be good, in which case we may be *tempted to pride*. So we must avoid two perils: complacency (we won't try) or pride (in our moral achievement). Here is the dilemma in Calvin's own words; notice that he formulates my simplified version ("If I can't be good . . .") in two separate antecedents, after his "(1)": ("When man is denied all uprightness . . ." and "because he is said to have no ability to pursue righteousness . . ."), each having essentially the same consequent, complacency:

> (1) When man is denied all uprightness, he immediately takes occasion for complacency from that fact; and, because he is said to have no ability to pursue righteousness on his own, he holds all such pursuit to be of no consequence, as if it did not pertain to him at all. (2) Nothing, however slight, can be credited to man without depriving God of his honor, and without man himself falling into ruin through brazen confidence. (2.2.1; the numbering is in the English text)

(1) Calvin's response to the first horn of the dilemma is singularly unconvincing. He simply asserts that those who have been taught to deny their own moral ability should be told nevertheless to seek the very goodness and freedom they lack. Then, as a second point, he adds that they will be even less complacent than if they already possessed the highest goodness and freedom. Here are Calvin's words:

> When a man has been taught that no good thing remains in his power, and that he is hedged about on all sides by most miserable necessity, in spite of this he should nevertheless be instructed to aspire to a good of which he is empty, to a freedom of which he has been deprived. In fact, he may thus be more sharply aroused from inactivity than if it were supposed that he was endowed with the highest virtues. (2.2.1; see also 2.2.10)

Let us look first at Calvin's first point, which is that a person who "has been taught that no good thing remains in his power. . . . in spite of this . . . should be instructed to aspire to a good of which he is empty, to a freedom of which he has been deprived." Calvin thinks he must defend this point because "too many persons have doubts about it." Well they might, of course, for how can a person who has come to see himself as having *no* moral goodness and as *incapable* of doing any good be motivated *at all* to perform any morally good activity? Motivation to do something good presupposes the belief that one *can* do it. But, says Calvin, we should be taught just the opposite of that belief, namely, that no "good thing is in [our] power." So how does Calvin remove the doubts on this first point? He doesn't, since he doesn't speak to the fairly self-evident proposition about motivation on which the doubts are based: what we are motivated to do or become depends on whether we believe we can do it or become what we want to become.

His second point is a still stronger claim than the first point. Not only can someone who denies his moral ability "be instructed to aspire to a good of which he is empty, to a freedom of which he has been deprived," and thereby be motivated out of complacency (first point); such a person "may thus be *more sharply aroused* from inactivity than if it were supposed that he was endowed with the highest virtues" (second point; emphasis mine). In other words, a person who sees no virtue in himself can be more strongly aroused to the performance of virtuous deeds than if he possessed the highest virtues. But certainly the possession of virtue is a necessary condition for the seeking and doing of good, so that this second case is even more improbable than the first. Strangely, however, Calvin thinks "everyone sees how necessary this second point is," so he offers no argument for it; while he argues against the first point, because he thinks "too many persons have doubts about it."

As Calvin continues his arguments against the first point, his confusion becomes evident. He even suggests that boasting might just be possible *without* denying the possession of something (supposedly good): "Since this is an undoubted fact, that nothing of his own ought to be taken away from man, it ought to be clearly evident how important it is for him to be barred from false boasting" (2.2.1). But instead of determining just what good "of his own" might survive in the fallen state, Calvin turns to a comparison between the fallen and created states with respect to pride: "When man was distinguished with the noblest marks of honor through God's beneficence, not even then was he permitted to boast about himself. How much more ought he now to humble himself, cast down as he has been—due to his own ungrateful-ness—from the loftiest glory into extreme disgrace" (2.2.1). This new argument seems to be: if it was forbidden us in our created state to boast about the eminent goodness we possessed in that state (since it was a gift from God), how much more it is forbidden in our fallen condition to boast (since we don't even have any goodness to boast about).

But the argument begs the very question at issue, whether or not there *is* any freedom and goodness left in our fallen condition, which would give us something to boast about. If Calvin's reference to the created state implies anything, it is that the pride of *fallen* humanity is as consistent with its possessing some moral freedom and goodness, as the pride that overcame *nonfallen* humanity is with its having possessed the moral freedom and goodness of its created state. In short, Calvin's warning against pride implies nothing by itself about the presence or absence of moral freedom and goodness. Hence, in order to deny that human beings retain some moral freedom and goodness after the fall, Calvin needs a premise quite different from his concern to warn against pride.

(2) Calvin's defense against the second horn of the dilemma is also unconvincing, because he trades on the ambiguity of our moral power being "credited to" us in the fallen state. If by this phrase he means arrogating such goodness to ourselves, to God's dishonor and to our own ruin, this horn of the dilemma stands; for it merely rephrases his warning against pride, which is: if you are proud, it will lead to your ruin. But then there would be no true dilemma. Calvin could simply affirm the second horn; it would not be linked to any claim about how much moral power or goodness persists in the fallen state. Calvin must therefore mean something different by the phrase being "credited to." He must mean to assert the opposite of the antecedent of the first horn. That horn was: "if we *deny* all moral ability in the fallen state." This horn must then mean: "if we *affirm* some moral ability in the fallen state."

This interpretation is supported by Augustine's original dilemma, which Calvin takes as his source. Augustine had argued: If I say I *can't* be good, I am in danger of complacency toward evil; whereas if I say I *can* be good, I am in danger of not asking God's help. Augustine rebuts this second horn by saying, simply: If I ask God's help (as I should), I won't be tempted to think I can be good (merely of my own powers).[2] Augustine's rebuttal has the great merit of allowing that human goodness can consistently be a matter of nature and of grace at once.

Calvin's rebuttal of this second horn, however, falters on the crucial ambiguity of his term, being "credited to." Notice how he moves from its first sense (we may not *arrogate* any goodness to ourselves) to its second (we may not *affirm* the *existence* of such goodness in ourselves): "Also, it is no less to our advantage than pertinent to God's glory that we be *deprived of all credit* for our wisdom and virtue. Thus those who *bestow upon us anything beyond the truth* add sacrilege to our ruin" (2.2.1; emphasis mine). That is, Calvin argues, we can avoid the dishonor of God that comes from "taking credit" for any ability to do good by free will by refusing to "bestow upon us anything beyond the truth." The argument leaves us none the wiser, however, about what, in truth, we *may* bestow on the natural will in its fallen state. We have already seen, of course, what Calvin believes this truth is: *no* inclination to moral goodness and *no* freedom to choose the good, and therefore no moral virtue.

That he really does believe this, and does so because of his concern about pride, is further evident from the concluding sentence of this opening section of chapter 2 that we have been discussing:

> It has been necessary to say this [that is, to argue as we have seen him do] by way of preface [to chapter 2] because some, while they hear that man's power is rooted out from its very foundations that God's power may be built up in man, bitterly loathe this whole disputation as dangerous, not to say superfluous. Nonetheless, it appears both fundamental in religion and most profitable to us.[3] (2.2.1)

It is, of course, "profitable" and "fundamental in religion" to warn against pride, the first and ultimate sin. My argument here is that Calvin is led by this entirely laudable point to a mistaken belief about the surviving natural powers of the will in the fallen state; it prevents him from examining these powers as they actually

99

exist, in accord with the Augustinian principle about "natural gifts."

Repeating the Confusion

Lest anyone suspect that my argument is based on just this one short section alone, I turn now to those later sections (10 and 11) in which Calvin reiterates his warnings against pride, with the same unfortunate consequence. After a lengthy polemical section (2–9) in which (as we have already discussed) he anticipates his later denials of free will and moral goodness, and before he turns to the main question of the condition of the intellect and the will in their fallen state, Calvin begins these two sections as follows:

> Nevertheless, what I mentioned at the beginning of this chapter I am compelled here to repeat once more: that whoever is utterly cast down and overwhelmed by the awareness of his calamity, poverty, nakedness, and disgrace has thus advanced farthest in knowledge of himself. For there is no danger of man's depriving himself of too much so long as he learns that in God must be recouped what he himself lacks. (2.2.10)

Is there "no danger of depriving himself of too much"?

It depends, of course, on the reference. If the reference is to the supernatural gifts, Calvin would be consistent, both with his doctrine of the bondage of the will and the Augustinian principle about supernatural gifts, in answering that such gifts have indeed been wholly lost. Doctrine and principle alike teach that the fall has deprived us of the ability to turn back in faith to God as our highest good and as the author of salvation. The question at issue in chapter 2 is, however, whether the *natural gift* of the will, which includes an inclination to goodness and freedom to pursue it, has been wholly lost. If Calvin's answer to this question is yes (as I have argued it is), he himself manifests the "danger of . . . depriving" human beings in their fallen state "of too much," since doctrine (the doctrine of creation) and principle (again, the Augustinian principle) alike require doing more justice to the will in its fallen state than he has done.

In the very next sentence Calvin gives himself an opening to examine just what qualities might "rightfully" belong to fallen human nature: "Yet he [fallen man] cannot claim for himself ever so little beyond what is rightfully his without losing himself in vain confidence and without usurping God's honor, and thus becoming guilty of monstrous sacrilege" (2.2.10). But he does not pause to define "what is rightfully his" in the fallen state.

The remainder of the section is given over to continued warnings against the "vain confidence" that "usurps God's honor." Jeremiah 17:5 is typical of the Scripture passages that Calvin quotes: "Cursed is the man who trusts man and makes flesh his arm." He summarizes: "All these passages have this purpose: that we should not rely on any opinion of our own strength, however small it is, if we want God to be favorable toward us, 'Who opposes the proud, but gives grace to the meek.'" Clearly, however, these passages only warn against the failure to trust in God; they do not speak to the question, what moral freedom and goodness remain in the fallen will, "however small it is."

The distinction between these two issues (the danger of pride and the extent of moral goodness in the fallen state) begs to be addressed in Calvin's closing comment on Isaiah 60:19. Isaiah writes: "The sun shall be no more your light by day, nor for brightness shall the moon give light to you by night; but the LORD will be your everlasting light." Comments Calvin: "Surely the Lord does not take away the brightness of the sun or moon from his servants; but because he wills alone to appear glorious in them, he calls them far away from trust even in those things which they deem most excellent." The parallel, which Calvin quite ignores, however, is (to use comparable language): "Surely the Lord does not take away the *natural* brightness of the human will, which persists in the fallen state; but because he wills to appear glorious in fallen human nature, he warns against any *trust* in such a thing that we could well deem most excellent." When Calvin finally tells us how much of the excellence of the human will is left in the fallen state, however, there is *nothing excellent in it*; it is nothing but a spontaneous inclination to evil.

Likewise, when he concludes section 11, Calvin ignores another opening he gives himself to discuss the natural gift of the will as it survives in the fallen state. This time the opening comes after quoting Augustine several times. A typical passage: "'Let no man flatter himself; of himself he is Satan. His blessing comes from God alone. For what do you have of your own but sin? Remove from yourself sin which is your own; for righteousness is of God'" (2.2.11). Augustine was nourished on the same rhetorical tradition as Calvin, and one can excuse the extravagance it produces, so long as it does not obscure the issue. It seems evident that Augustine here, and Calvin in citing him, refers to the loss of our supernatural gifts; it is the only sense that can be given Calvin's comment: "God so commends his grace to us that we know that we are nothing. By God's mercy alone we stand, since by ourselves we are nothing but evil."

But shortly after this, as if for a moment checking himself, Calvin says this:

> Now I do not claim that man, unconvinced, should yield himself voluntarily, and that, if he has any powers, he should turn his mind from them in order that he may be subjected to true humility. But I require only that, laying aside the disease of self-love and ambition, by which he is blinded and thinks more highly of himself than he ought, he rightly recognize himself in the faithful mirror of Scripture. (2.2.11)

But what "powers" are they, that we should not "turn our mind from them" in order to maintain a proper humility? Perhaps Calvin here refers to the natural powers of intellect and will, which he is about to discuss in the rest of chapter 2. Yet he constantly denies, here and elsewhere, that there is such power, at least in the fallen will, and suggests that this denial follows from the moral need to avoid pride. That it does not so follow should be plain. To avoid reliance on one's own goodness does not require that one denies it; indeed, it is more likely that any warning against self-reliance *presupposes* some moral ability in the fallen state, on which one might be tempted to rely.

Concluding Reflections on Calvin's Reasoning

Is it understandable that Calvin should fall into this reasoning? Not once we take a close look. Consider his argument. The sin of arrogance, of relying upon ourselves alone, is the sin that brought us to our fall. Such pride continues to plague our fallen state; in fact, it is now our besetting sin, the one we need most to confess and repent of, the one that most prevents our conversion, our accepting the gospel. So our primary concern in the fallen state is to avoid relying on any moral goodness of our own, for that will fly in the face of grace. Grace alone can save us; indeed, it offers the gift of a moral goodness—true righteousness—that we have lost. Therefore, we must deny that we possess any moral goodness or moral choice whatsoever, on pain of missing the grace of God that alone can rescue us from our fallen state.

The fallacy in the argument is that it fails to distinguish between two kinds of moral freedom and goodness, between the *natural* and the *supernatural* gifts identified in the Augustinian principle. What if there really is a level of moral goodness and free choice in the will that persists as a "natural gift" into the fallen state, even though, of course, both are now corrupted by the very arrogance that caused the fall? Why cannot such corrupted moral goodness and free choice still *be* moral goodness and free choice? If so, Calvin's unqualified conclusion that there is no goodness or freedom whatsoever in the fallen state does not follow, either from our loss of the supernatural gift of the highest moral goodness and freedom or from the prohibition against pride and self-reliance that is always relevant, to both fallen and redeemed states of humanity.

I have already suggested that the Augustinian principle not only permits but requires that some moral goodness and free will persist in the fallen state. If this is correct, to recognize such goodness and free will in fallen human beings will not threaten the necessity of grace for conversion. The first and most important effect of such grace is to restore the supernatural goodness that we have indeed lost; included in this special goodness will be humility itself, which undercuts our pride and motivates us to praise God from whom *all* blessings flow—blessings of the nature with which we were created and blessings of the salvation which grace restores. In addition, such restoration of faith and piety heals the corruption of our natural powers and strengthens the will's free choices of good over evil. Just how this healing works and how much of it we can expect in this life are further questions, which, like the others I am raising in this book, need more development than they have received in the Reformed tradition to date.

On the corrected scenario I propose, the necessary exhortation against pride would go like this. Given the persistence (not loss) in the fallen state of the natural components of the will, namely, its inclination to goodness and power of choice between good and evil (although they are now corrupted), we are to be warned against the pride and self-assurance that led to the first sin in the state of integrity, for that pride is still our besetting sin. Moreover, our plight in this fallen state is far worse than it was in the created state. There we enjoyed the supernatural gift of faith, even though it was not supported by an irresistible grace like the grace proffered to us now, if we believe the gospel. But if our inordinate self-assurance in that state of integrity led to our fall, how much more will such self-assurance in the fallen state prevent our turning back (our conversion) to God, based as such self-assurance might well be on the very natural gifts of moral goodness and free choice we still possess? For God alone gives us whatever natural freedom and goodness we still enjoy, even though we have corrupted them; therefore, he alone deserves the honor, thanksgiving, and praise for them, which we are apt, in our fallen condition, to arrogate to ourselves.

Indeed, Calvin's claim that we must deny all moral goodness and free choice as part of our way back to God actually invites an error exactly opposite to the one with which he charges his opponents. The latter error is that "those who bestow upon us anything beyond the truth [as Calvin sees it] add sacrilege to our ruin" (2.2.1). But Calvin's own error is to bestow on us *too little*, when he denies such moral goodness and freedom of choice as we still possess in our fallen state. That error is also, in its own way, tantamount to denying God, since it denies his goodness in the *nature* of human beings in their fallen state; it is a denial that prevents our thanking him for that very goodness. For how can we thank God for such goodness if, in Calvin's own words, we are "taught that no good thing remains in [their] power"? We cannot, of course, but that is the unhappy consequence of Calvin's rejection of the created freedom and moral goodness of the will insofar as it survives in its fallen state.

So what should Calvin have done instead? He should have *begun* his whole discussion in chapter 2 with the Augustinian principle, with which he frames his discussion, and stuck to an analysis of just what the natural will lost in the fall and just what it retained, in spite of its being corrupted, in the fallen state. There was no need for him to utter more than an occasional warning against pride, let alone to connect that warning so intimately and misleadingly with the issue at hand. It is too late to ask Calvin to avoid the reasoning that leads to his defective account of the fallen will, but not too late for his followers to avoid that reasoning and develop a remedy for its unhappy results. In the next chapter I want to take the first step in that direction.

Doesn't Grace Presuppose Nature?

By this time it should be evident that the question whether the will in its fallen state possesses any moral uprightness and free choice between good and evil is an issue of substance. Surprisingly, however, Calvin turns it into a merely verbal matter. Still motivated by his overriding concern to warn against pride, he writes:

> But how few men are there, I ask, who when they hear free will attributed to man do not immediately conceive him to be master of his own mind and will, able of his own power to turn himself toward either good or evil? Yet (someone will say) this sort of danger will be removed if the common folk are diligently warned of its meaning. Man's disposition voluntarily so inclines to falsehood that he more quickly derives error from one word than truth from a wordy discourse. In this very word we have more certain experience of this matter than we should like. For, overlooking that interpretation of the ancient writers, almost all their successors, while they have clung to the etymological meaning of the word, have been carried into a ruinous self-assurance. (2.2.7)

To avoid such "ruinous self-assurance," then, Calvin urges his fellow theologians to banish the term *free will,* resolving to do just that himself: "But

I hold that, because it cannot be retained without great peril, it will . . . be a great boon for the church if it be abolished. I prefer not to use it myself, and I should like others, if they seek my advice, to avoid it" (2.2.8).[1]

As I see it, Calvin's proposal here is a mistake. Whether the will is still free in more than Calvin's minimalist sense and whether it possesses some genuine level of moral goodness apart from conversion are issues of great importance. I want now to propose a remedy to what I see as Calvin's faulty views. The remedy has been implicit in my discussions over the last two chapters and it can now be formulated simply and briefly. It reflects the two points of the Augustinian principle as well as the teachings of Scripture and human experience, the experience of both Christian believers and fallen human beings alike.

The Augustinian Principle

First, then, Reformed theologians and philosophers, contrary to their mentor, should affirm the free choice of the will since, as an essential component of human nature as God created it, such choice could not be destroyed or lost by the fall. By free choice is meant the natural capacity for contrary choice between the morally good and evil alternatives with which the course of human life and action is now filled, together with the possibility of exercising this capacity for the development of moral virtues and vices. These capacities, both for moral choice and moral virtue, have been corrupted by the fall; still they are supported in a great variety of ways, degrees, and circumstances by God's common grace. The effect of this grace, then, is not only to restrain evil choices and human vices but also to preserve and promote the functioning of the will according to the nature God bestowed upon it, with respect to moral action and the development of moral character, in spite of the corrupting influences of sin. And, as a corollary to this first point and likewise included in the doctrine of common grace, Reformed thinkers should also affirm the will's persistent natural inclination to moral goodness, even amidst the conflict that has set in between this inclination and the new inclination to moral evil that now limits, opposes, and debilitates the original inclination to goodness.

Second, in accord with the second point of the Augustinian principle, Reformed thinkers will still continue to emphasize the inability of the will, in spite of its persisting inclination to goodness and capacity for moral choice, to convert itself back into the favor of God, since the supernatural gifts required for this conversion have indeed been lost by the fall and depend for their restoration upon the special saving and regenerating grace of God. By making this distinction between the created nature of the will and the supernatural gifts required for its redemption from its fallen state, the Reformed view can be brought more consistently into line with the Augustinian principle than Calvin has managed to do. With this distinction in hand, moreover, Reformed thinkers can still follow their mentor in his conspicuous warnings against pride. The warning will be pertinent to every state of the will: whether simply fallen, or fallen but hearing the gospel, or having heard the gospel coming to faith, or having come to faith, striving to persevere in it. Finally, by making this distinction, Reformed theologians and philosophers will be able to give an intelligible account of the moral virtue (and vice) of human beings in their fallen condition, which Calvin is unable to do. Let me now elaborate on this last point, since it looks in the direction of giving an account of the universal human experience of the difference between human virtue and vice.

The Moral Virtues (and Vices) of Fallen Humanity

In spite of his repeated denials of the moral freedom and goodness of the fallen will, Calvin still recognizes the moral virtues of fallen human beings, even though such recognitions are rare and comparatively brief. In one passage, however, he discusses such virtues at length and actually seems to attribute it to the *nature* of fallen human beings:

> In every age there have been persons who, guided by *nature*, have striven toward virtue throughout life. I have nothing to say against them even if many lapses can be noted in their moral conduct. For they have by the very zeal of their honesty given proof that

there was some purity in their *nature*. . . . These examples, accordingly, seem to warn us against adjudging man's *nature* wholly corrupted, because some men have by its prompting not only excelled in remarkable deeds, but conducted themselves most honorably throughout life. But here it ought to occur to us that amid this corruption of nature there is some place for God's grace; not such grace as to cleanse it, but to restrain it inwardly. (2.3.3 emphasis mine)

Here Calvin makes an important qualification, missing in most of his other discussions. Here he suggests that the fallen will has *natural capacities* for virtues and good deeds after all. He introduces the concept of nature here only, however, to have it disappear in favor of grace at the end of the passage. We have already seen in chapter 3 that Calvin has no *theory* of the natural components of the fallen human will that can even begin to account for its production of good deeds, let alone moral virtue. For if, as we there saw, all the natural inclinations of the fallen will are evil, there can be no moral virtue at all. The very idea of a moral virtue is of an inner disposition, an *inclination*, to pursue virtuous deeds.

It will not do to say that Calvin accounts for these virtues and good deeds as gifts of divine grace. He does that, of course, at the end of the quoted passage, and later Reformed theologians have developed the doctrine of "common grace" on the basis of passages like this one.[2] I shall discuss the doctrine further in a moment. The problem that needs to be faced, however, is that attributing these virtues to such nonsaving grace sheds no light on *how* the fallen will itself *functions* as a *natural power* to *produce* the good deeds and virtues that Calvin refers to. If the Augustinian principle is correct, enough of the created will must survive in the fallen state to provide the basis for a general theory of human moral agency. That the will is corrupted is evident enough from the testimony of both experience and Scripture. That it is completely dependent upon the divine grace of regeneration for being restored to God is also clearly taught in Scripture. The question is, does anything of the will's natural inclination to moral goodness and capacity for moral choice persist in the fallen state, in spite of the corruption it brought upon itself in the fall?

Scripture on Human Nature

The remedy I propose, that such a natural moral capacity continues to exist in the fallen state, can be supported from Scripture, as well as experience. The classic text is from St. Paul, though he hardly elaborates on it as a theologian or philosopher is expected to do:

> When Gentiles who have not the law do by nature what the law requires, they are a law unto themselves, even though they do not have the law. They show that what the law requires is written on their hearts, while their conscience also bears witness and their conflicting thoughts accuse or perhaps excuse them. (Rom. 2:14–15 RSV)

Here Paul gives us a picture of fallen human *nature* that is still capable of doing what the law requires. It is of utmost importance to notice that Paul says that it is by *nature*, not by grace, that the moral law is "written" on the human heart, and in such a way that human beings not only know what is right, but also can follow or not follow it; for it will both accuse them when they do wrong and excuse them when they do right. This accusing and excusing suggests further that the fallen conscience still faces the choice between doing good or evil.

So much for choice. What about motivation? Can there still be a natural motivation to moral goodness in the fallen will, granted, of course, that the will is now corrupted by the fall and quite deprived of the supernatural gifts, as these are defined in the Augustinian principle? The answer has to be yes; for it is the most reasonable interpretation of the Pauline language. The burden of proof is on Calvin to defend his view that the fall reduced the nature of the will as God created it to a spontaneous and exclusive pursuit of evil. Calvin himself acknowledges, as we saw in chapter 2, that God created the will with *both components* as essential to its nature: an inclination to goodness and the power of choice between good and evil.

Calvin's claim that human beings in their primal disobedience destroyed the very components of their wills as God created them seems quite improbable. If by our fall we could have reduced the created nature of the will to nothing but a spontaneous inclination to evil, God gave us an extraordinary power indeed: the power, by exercising our choice between good and evil, to utterly destroy that power as he created it, just in case we chose evil, even the worst evil itself of disobeying him. Scripture nowhere suggests that human beings were created with that kind of power. Or at least Calvin nowhere attempts to show that it does. Indeed, Calvin's own affirmation of the Augustinian principle implies that he senses the absurdity of interpreting the result of the primal disobedience that way. Moreover, as we saw in chapter 2, Calvin even insists that the loss of the supernatural gifts was a loss of something "adventitious, and beyond nature." Why does he use such language, unless he wants to preserve the *nature* of the intellect and will as these persist in the midst of their corruption in the fallen state?

In spite of this, Calvin interprets the Pauline passage from Romans in a way that reflects his defective account of the human will instead of his commitment to the Augustinian principle. He claims first that Paul's main point is to show that fallen human beings are inexcusable for their wrongdoing: "The purpose of natural law, therefore, is to render man inexcusable" (2.2.22; see also 3.19.15). The context supports this first claim, for Paul emphasizes our inexcusability before God already in 1:18–20 before he repeats it in the first verse of chapter 2.

Calvin goes on to claim that by the term *heart* Paul refers here only to the intellect and not to the will, but without arguing the point here in the *Institutes*. In his *Commentary*, however, he writes:

> There is no basis for deducing the power of the will from the present passage, as if Paul had said that the keeping of the law is within our power, for he does not speak of our power to fulfil the law, but of our knowledge of it. The word *hearts* is not to be taken for the seat of the affections, but simply for the understanding, as in Deut. 29:4, "The Lord hath not given you a heart to know," and in Luke 24.25, "O foolish men, and slow of heart to believe."[3]

But this second claim, that Paul here refers only to moral *knowledge*, not also to moral *inclination* or *ability*, is not evident from the text or context. We have already noted that the scope of the scriptural concept of *heart* often includes the functions of both the intel-

lect and the will; and we have noted Calvin's own tendency to asso-
ciate that concept more with the will than with the intellect (chapter 1, n. 1). So his claim that Paul's language here has nothing to
do with the will is hardly obvious. How could Paul say that Gentiles sometimes "do by nature what the law requires," if such doing
did not involve the inclinations and choices of the will?

Of course, because of the fall the Gentiles do not fulfill the law
perfectly (neither do believers); but it hardly follows that they have
no moral ability at all to follow the law. St. Paul's language is thus
more open to permitting the survival of intellect *and will* in the
fallen state than Calvin admits; he seems moved to this second
claim more by his own diminished view of the will than by an
objective analysis of "doing by *nature* what the law requires."

It should be clear that, by the remedy to Calvin's views, which
I have now outlined and which I think Romans 2:14–15 supports,
I do not intend to imply that there is, after the fall, a realm of
"pure nature" in human life, thought, and action that is essentially unimpaired and unaffected by the restoration of faith and
true piety in a converted human being. I agree with the long-
standing Protestant objection to a "two-story" relationship
between nature and grace, on which grace is merely added (the
superadditum donum) to a human nature that requires little or no
internal healing from the effects of sin. Arvin Vos has argued,
however, that this objection is directed against a later (sixteenth-
and seventeenth-century) corruption within Catholic thought,
which entered it under the spell of the new humanist, Cartesian,
and later Enlightenment views of an autonomous conception of
reason and will. Vos also shows that Aquinas, at least, teaches a
properly qualified version of the moral virtue that persists after
the fall; in this version such moral virtue is not only wounded by
sin, but also lacks the important ingredient of being directed to
God, a characteristic of the will which depends on the presence
of the supernatural gifts given only by saving grace.[4]

An Example

In his discussion of Catiline and Camillus, Calvin provides his
own best example of how his diminished concept of the will leads

113

him to an incoherent account of the moral goodness of fallen humanity. Says Calvin: "Either we must make Camillus equal to Catiline, or we shall have in Camillus an example proving that nature, if carefully cultivated, is not utterly devoid of goodness" (2.3.4). He opts for the second alternative: "Indeed, I admit that the endowments resplendent in Camillus were gifts of God and seem rightly commendable in themselves." But then Calvin undermines the "splendor" of these gifts he has just acknowledged when he asks, "But how will these serve as proofs of *natural* goodness in him?" (emphasis mine). His answer is, they do not: "Even in the loftiest appearance of integrity, [human nature] is always found to be impelled toward corruption." He concludes: "Therefore as you will not commend a man for virtue when his vices impress you under the appearance of virtues, so you will not attribute to the human will the capability of seeking after the right so long as the will remains set in its own perversity" (2.3.4). Thus what Calvin begins by calling "gifts of God" he ends by rejecting as the mere "appearance" of virtue that conceals a will "set in its own perversity." Instead of invoking "common grace" to explain the persistence of a *divinely created natural will,* Calvin writes: "These are not common gifts of nature, but the special graces of God, which he bestows variously and in a certain measure upon men otherwise wicked." Hence "anything in profane men that appears praiseworthy must be considered worthless" (2.3.4).

One could argue that Calvin is making the point here that Camillus with all his admirable virtues is as far from conversion as Catiline with all his terrible vices. Such an argument finds some support, perhaps, in Calvin's conclusion to the section: "As for the virtues that deceive us with their vain show, they shall have their praise in the political assembly and in common renown among men; but before the heavenly judgment seat they shall be of no value to acquire righteousness" (2.3.4). Even if this argument is correct, however, it is irrelevant; for it obscures the moral difference between fallen human beings, which is the whole point of the example. Recall (in the passage cited earlier) how Calvin introduces the whole discussion: "In every age there have been persons who, guided by *nature*, have striven toward virtue throughout life. I have nothing to say against them even if many lapses can be noted in their moral conduct. For they have by the very zeal of their honesty given proof that there was some purity in their *nature*" (2.3.3; emphasis mine).

It is unfortunate that Calvin mixes together two distinct issues in this chapter: first, what elements of the natural will's moral capacity survive in the fallen state and second, whether the capacities of the will that do survive can assist in or conduce toward its conversion. It seems evident that Calvin turns the inability of the will to restore itself to favor with God into a theory of a will that is unable to produce any moral good at all.

Similarly, Calvin's polemical remarks about conversion in the sections directly following his discussion of Camillus and Catiline are irrelevant to the question whether any natural components of the will survive the fall. These polemics recall his earlier attack on Lombard for a "hint that man by his very own nature somehow seeks after the good," so that "we cooperate with the assisting grace of God" (2.2.6). Calvin rejects the notion that our natural but corrupted will can "prepare" us for conversion (2.3.7). He believes that both ideas—cooperation and preparation— undermine the complete dependence of the will upon saving grace for conversion.

But, again, even if such attacks are justified in order to maintain the dependence of the will upon saving grace for conversion, they give us no theory of the fallen will itself, which would explain the significant differences between the moral character of fallen human beings. Invoking a doctrine of common grace sheds no light on how the will produces various degrees of moral virtue (and vice) in fallen human beings. For that, Calvin needs a theory of the interaction between the intellect (knowledge of good and evil) and will (with its good and evil inclinations and its capacity for contrary choice). But Calvin provides no such theory; or rather, he provides only a minimalist theory of the will, on which it is inclined exclusively to evil and incapable of any morally good choice. But this theory is quite incapable of explaining the moral difference between Camillus and Catiline.

Common Grace

Clearly this attenuated view of the fallen will dictates Calvin's equally attenuated theory of common grace. It is a grace that is restricted to *restraining* the evil inclinations of the will (there are no good ones for it to sustain) and producing right actions that are only *externally* right. Actions that are only externally right are those that conform to the moral law but are performed without the proper moral motivation that would make them virtuous:

> If every soul is subject to such abominations as the apostle boldly declares, we surely see what would happen if the Lord were to permit human lust to wander according to its own inclination. No mad beast would rage as unrestrainedly; no river, however swift and violent, burst so madly into flood. In the elect the Lord cures these diseases in a way that we shall soon explain. Others he merely restrains by throwing a bridle over them only that they may not break loose, inasmuch as he foresees their control to be expedient to preserve all that is. Hence some are restrained by *shame* from breaking out into many kinds of foulness, others by the *fear* of the law—even though they do not, for the most part, hide their impurity. Still others, because they consider an honest manner of life *profitable*, in some measure aspire to it. Others rise above the common lot, in order by their excellence to *keep the rest obedient* to them. Thus God by his providence bridles perversity of nature, that it may not break forth into action; but he does not purge it within. (2.3.3; emphasis mine)

Whether actions are right or wrong, they are all motivated by evil impulses (since these are the only kind possessed by the fallen will)—impulses like shame, fear, selfish advantage, and the lust for power. The fallen will is entirely without such good impulses as courage, cooperation, honesty, loyalty, and the sense of duty itself.

This picture of fallen human nature is bleak indeed. Calvin is not alone, of course, in painting such an utterly dark picture of human nature and motivation; similar portraits emerge in non-Christian thinkers as well, from the ancient sophists to modern philosophers like Thomas Hobbes, Immanuel Kant, and Jean-Paul Sartre.[5] The question is whether this utterly dark picture is the whole truth, and whether it is the only one that Scripture can be quoted to support.

This bleak conception of human nature, conjoined with the doctrine of common grace, has remained essentially unchanged in the Reformed theological tradition since Calvin introduced it. For example, Louis Berkhof, whose *Systematic Theology* has been widely used and very influential during the last half century, asks: "How can we account for it that sinful man still retains some knowledge of God, of natural things, and of the difference between good and evil, and shows some regard for virtue and for good outward behavior?"[6] Berkhof's answer: "common grace," which only "curbs the destructive power of sin [and] maintains in a measure the moral order of the universe, thus making an orderly life possible . . . Common grace . . . never removes the guilt of sin, does not renew human nature, but only has a restraining effect on the corrupting influence of sin and in a measure mitigates its results."[7]

I suggested a moment ago that Calvin's view of fallen human nature dictates the scope of his concept of common grace. That is, it does not seem that Calvin first had a theory of common grace, from which he then derived his theory of human nature. Instead, he first developed his theory of human nature, and more particularly, of the will after the fall. But since that theory of the fallen will as inclined to nothing but evil hardly squares with human experience, he then invokes a theory of nonsaving, divine grace to explain why human beings do not appear as bad as his account of the will implies they should be.[8] The point is important, for it suggests that if there is a more adequate account of the fallen will than Calvin provides, there should also be a correlative modification in his doctrine of common grace. That, at any rate, is what I also propose.

A corrected view of the fallen will requires a broadened concept of common grace.

A Difficult Passage

Before turning to that broadened concept of common grace, however, I will give another example of how a more adequate view of the will could have kept Calvin from serious confusion. Had Calvin developed a more positive account of the fallen will, one that reflects both the biblical doctrine of creation and the Augustinian principle he avows, he could have avoided writing the following passage at the beginning of the nine sections that he devotes explicitly to conversion. Much commented on by Calvin scholars, it is important to analyze, since its confusions are echoed throughout the ensuing discussion. Here is the passage:

> If, therefore, a stone is transformed into flesh when God converts us to zeal for the right, whatever is of our own will is effaced. What takes its place is wholly from God. I say that the will is effaced; not in so far as it is will, for in man's conversion what belongs to his primal nature remains entire. I also say that it is created anew; not meaning that the will now begins to exist, but that it is changed from an evil will to a good will. I affirm that this is wholly God's doing.[9](2.3.6)

The confusions are obvious. Calvin's analogy of the unconverted will to a stone implies that the entire will suffers from the same bondage that characterizes its specific loss of the spiritual gifts. He suggests further that no moral zeal, no moral motivation for what is right, is possible among human beings apart from conversion; that conversion presupposes nothing but evil inclinations in the fallen will; and that in converting the will, God both creates it anew, yet finds it already existing with the nature he gave it.

Had Calvin preserved the natural components of the will amidst their corruption, he would have been able to avoid these confusions in the following way. He would not have said that God, in converting us, *effaces* the very will he created, but rather, that he enables it to exercise *again* the "supernatural gifts" of faith, piety, and the love of God that it exercised before the Fall. These are the gifts that are created "anew," not the will itself; for they are "created" (or, why not say "restored"?) as functions of the two *natural* components of the will, namely, its inclination to goodness and its freedom of choice (which *are* created, in the proper sense of that term). Formulating the divine activity of conversion in this way would have the further advantage of integrating the supernatural gifts with the "primal nature" of the will,

118

which "remains entire," even as God created it. The grace of regeneration thus does not create the *will* anew, but restores several specific *exercises* of the will that it lost, like faith in God and love of him as its highest good.

Calvin's Own Model

For further support of my remedy of Calvin's minimalist account of the fallen will, I appeal to the model he himself offers when he turns his attention from the fallen will to the fallen intellect. At that transition, he not only repeats the Augustinian distinction between natural and supernatural gifts (2.2.12) that he has introduced earlier (2.2.4), but also reiterates it well into his discussion of the intellect (2.2.16). Even more striking is what he does *not* do. He nowhere argues from the danger of pride to a *denial* of the genuine natural capacities of the intellect as they manifest themselves in the fallen state. Instead of any rather wholesale rejection of its ability to seek and find the truth, comparable to his rejection of the will's ability to seek and achieve goodness, he carefully distinguishes between two kinds of understanding in the fallen state, *earthly* and *heavenly*:

> This, then, is the distinction: that there is one kind of understanding of earthly things; another of heavenly. I call "earthly things" those which do not pertain to God or his Kingdom, to true justice, or to the blessedness of the future life; but which have their significance and relationship with regard to the present life and are, in a sense, confined within its bounds. I call "heavenly things" the pure knowledge of God, the nature of true righteousness, and the mysteries of the Heavenly Kingdom. (1.2.13)

Calvin acknowledges an ability in the intellect to know even the "heavenly things": "It is intelligent enough to taste something of things above, although it is more careless about investigating these" (2.2.13). This acknowledgment is not surprising, of course; for the inexcusability Calvin ascribes to human beings for turning away from God in their fallen condition presupposes that the intellect retains a sufficient knowledge of God to warrant such inexcusability (see also 1.3; 4).

Moreover, Calvin goes out of his way to delineate and emphasize the scope of the fallen intellect's ability for earthly things, however restricted it is by the noetic effects of sin. His eloquence on the achievements of reason in the arts and sciences is well known. "Whenever we come upon these matters in secular writers, let that admirable light of truth shining in them teach us that the mind of man, though fallen and perverted from his wholeness, is nevertheless clothed and ornamented with God's excellent gifts"[10] (2.2.15). But he offers no comparable encomium on "the admirable light of goodness shining in the moral deeds of fallen human beings" (to imitate his own language). Why does Calvin not see the fallen will, analogously, as capable of producing gifts of moral goodness comparable to the excellent gifts of truth produced by the fallen intellect?

A similar question may be asked with respect to Calvin's familiar admonition: "If we regard the Spirit of God as the sole fountain of truth, we shall neither reject the truth itself, nor despise it wherever it shall appear, unless we wish to dishonor the Spirit of God" (2.2.13).[11] The question is, why has Calvin no parallel admonition neither to reject moral goodness nor to despise it wherever it appears among fallen human beings, even apart from conversion, lest we dishonor the natural gifts for such goodness that God has given, including freedom of the will? The disparity between Calvin's great appreciation of the arts and sciences and his almost total lack of appreciation of moral goodness in the fallen state stems directly from his faulty concept of the fallen will.

Nature and Grace

To elaborate on a point made earlier, it is important to emphasize that Calvin saw no conflict between describing all the activities of the fallen intellect in the arts and sciences as "natural gifts," while in the same breath attributing them to (common) grace: "Yet so universal is this good that every man ought to recognize for himself in it the peculiar grace of God" (2.2.14; see also 17). Calvin could easily have done the same for the natural gifts of the fallen will, its inclination to goodness (not only to evil), its capacity to choose good deeds (not only eviduce moral virtues (not only vices), had he simply recognized these natural gifts as such, as survivals in the fallen state of some of the moral goodness and freedom that characterized the will as it was originally created.[12]

As a matter of fact, we find more traces of Calvin's recognition of such positive moral goodness in several of the sections dealing explicitly with the intellect than in the many devoted explicitly to the will. For example, Calvin acknowledges both that fallen human beings are still social and political animals and that they can frame their earthly lives in accord with the second table of the law. The principles of justice that are necessary for political order are "implanted in all men" (2.2.13; see also 2.2.24). And, having cited Romans 2:14–15, he admits "there is nothing more common than for a man to be sufficiently instructed in a right standard of conduct by natural law" (2.2.22).

These acknowledgments of natural goodness appear properly enough in Calvin's discussion of the intellect; why does he not continue to discuss them when he turns to the will? More to the point, why does he not *connect* this natural goodness to the *natural functions* of the will? It is precisely this connection, however, between human goodness in its fallen state (and the moral order it produces) and the natural components of the will from which this goodness arises, that is missing in Calvin's account. This gap in his moral psychology suggests that the moral and political goodness of human beings in their fallen state stems from the intellect alone, without being processed by the free choice of the will in accord with its natural inclination for goodness and natural capacity for moral choice.

In short, just as Calvin recognizes that there is an area of "earthly life" in which the intellectual powers continue to function amidst the corruption of the fall, without its being able to function properly in the area of "heavenly things," so also he should have shown how the same is true for the fallen will. But he didn't. The essence of my proposal is that his followers today should begin to make up for this mistake.

The Appeal to Augustine

I could extend this chapter by commenting on Calvin's appeal to Augustine in support of his minimalist view of the fallen will (see for example 2.3.13–14) and by examining his numerous "Refutations of the Objections Commonly Put Forward in Defense of Free Will" (2.5). But he makes no further claims in these refutations that are not in need of the remedy I have proposed, and there is little point for my purposes here in showing that Augustine's account of the fallen will, where Calvin appeals to it, may require the same remedy.

My remedy presupposes the truth of the "Augustinian principle" itself, that it is one thing to recognize the helplessness of the fallen will to regain, by conversion, the supernatural gifts it has lost, but quite another to deny wholesale the persistence in its fallen state of the two natural components of the will with which God endowed it in creation: an inclination to moral goodness and a capacity for contrary moral choice. Nothing that Calvin or Augustine says in support of the former dependence of the will upon regenerating grace requires us to reject the survival of the created nature of the will into the fallen state, in spite of the corruption that now plagues it.

That Augustine does more than Calvin, however, to safeguard the freedom of the will in its fallen state could no doubt be shown; in support of this claim I here content myself to repeat a quotation from A. N. S. Lane, which I cited at the beginning of this study (Introduction):

> Calvin's teaching on freewill is very close to that of Augustine. Perhaps the greatest difference is one of attitude. Augustine, while clearly teaching the bondage of the will and the sovereignty of grace, took great care to preserve man's freewill. Calvin was much more polemical in his assertion of human impotence and was reluctant to talk of freewill. What Augustine had carefully safeguarded, Calvin grudgingly conceded.[13]

I have argued that Calvin does not even "grudgingly concede" the freedom of the will in its full-bodied sense as an inclination to goodness (as well as evil) and the ability to choose between them with respect to "earthly things." It is sufficient for my purpose to note that the "Augustinian principle" itself was so named, long before Calvin invoked it only to ignore it, by earlier Scholastics. They so named it because they believed that it reflected the great Latin Church Father's conviction that human nature, no less than regenerating grace, originates in the goodness of God and must therefore be given its full due in any account of its fallen state by Christian theologians and philosophers. Reformed thinkers, correcting their mentor, should do the same.

Epilogue: The Future Direction of Reformed Thought on the Will

I have sometimes made it sound as if Calvin should have given a different account of both the created and the fallen will from the one we find in his writings. That, of course, is a foolish wish. Still, it is an understandable desire in the face of the embarrassment that Calvin's deficient account of the will ought to provoke in those who have otherwise been inspired by Calvin's greatness as a Protestant Reformer of the church and its theology. The best (and only) move left is to face Calvin's mistakes and correct them. Let me close my discussion, then, by summarizing these mistakes and the remedies I propose, review the significance of these remedies, and indicate the direction a Reformed theory of the will should take, especially for the development of Reformed epistemology.

Mistakes, Remedies, and Their Significance

There can be no doubt that a consistent Reformed account of the will requires a voluntarist account of the human will not only in its fallen and redeemed states, but also as God originally created it. But Calvin begins his discussion of the created will with an intellectualist account of it. Fortunately, it is clear that he ends by presupposing a voluntarist view, so that the remedy is easy to apply. It consists in amending his earlier account, which claims that the will always follows the right leading of the intellect, with his later account, which implies that the will sometimes does not follow this leading and can even be the cause of the intellect's proposing the very choices between good and evil that invite its choice of the evil alternative.

The great advantage of this voluntarist correction is that it provides one of the necessary conditions of the guilt entailed by human wrongdoing, namely, that the will is the original source of that wrongdoing; it is not due to a failure in the intellect. Indeed, the intellect's knowledge of right and wrong, which is the other condition for guilt, survives in the fallen state, since like the will it is a natural gift of the created state and cannot, therefore, be destroyed by any defection of the will. On that point, Calvin is clear and even emphatic. Even though the knowledge of good and evil is diminished in certain ways by the fall and some of this is due to the will itself, which typically seeks to avert the intellect from its own testimony about good and evil, the intellect's knowledge of right and wrong (and even of God himself in the *sensus divinitatis*) remains sufficiently present to accuse fallen human beings of their willful defection from God. Hence their wrongdoing is essentially more deliberate than not and they are without excuse. But what about the fallen will? Has the will as God created it, with a natural inclination to goodness and capacity for choice between good and evil, persisted into the fallen state? Calvin's answer to this question, I have argued, is mistaken. For though he holds that God created the will with these two components, he holds that neither of these components has survived the fall. What has survived is only the inclination of the will, but it is an inclination for nothing but evil.

This claim departs from the "Augustinian principle" that Calvin himself invokes, which distinguishes between the supernatural gifts that were lost in the fall and the natural gifts that were not. Calvin rightly teaches that the inclination to faith in God and the capacity to choose this faith and its consequent acts of pious worship, service, praise, and thanksgiving to God are indeed lost and can be regained only by saving grace. His claim, however, that the fallen will is inclined to nothing but evil is mistaken and must be remedied by accepting that both the will's inclination to moral goodness and its capacity to choose it over evil survive in the fallen state. Of course, because of the fall, this residual inclination to moral goodness must now struggle against inclinations to evil, a condition that also corrupts its choices between good and evil. But in this state of moral conflict and corruption, the natural goodness and freedom of the will are still evident. As a result, human life, in spite of its pervasive moral corruption, not to mention its many moral atrocities, still manifests signs of moral goodness and even splendor, at least with respect to what Calvin identifies as "earthly things."

Human life is sustained in this goodness by a *common grace* that God shows toward the human beings he has created. But Reformed thinkers will need to expand the scope of this grace to reflect the survival of these natural components of the will. The traditional Reformed doctrine of common grace, on which it only restrains evil inclinations and secures only an external conformity of human acts with the moral law, is insufficient.

In developing these remedies for the defects in Calvin's account of the will, Reformed thinkers should henceforth follow the lead of Scotistic voluntarism for understanding the created relationship between intellect and will; and for a theory of the fallen will they should follow the model Calvin himself provides in his much more generous account of the fallen intellect. They will thereby do more justice to the natural, created components of the will as these persist into the fallen state than either Calvin or the Reformed tradition has done. For in so doing, they will affirm that the fallen will still possesses by its nature the two components with which God created it, an inclination to moral goodness and the ability to choose between following this inclination and the new inclinations to evil that now corrupt its nature in the fallen state. Even its best moral choices, of course, will not be properly directed to God unless the will is converted, nor will they avail for its conversion, that is, for the restoration of the "supernatural gifts" of faith in God and love for him that were lost in the fall. The restoration of these gifts depends upon a regeneration of the will as an act of the saving grace of God.

The advantages of these remedies are several. First, they open the way to a more coherent Reformed account of the universal human testimony to the human moral struggle than is presently possible on Calvin's account of the fallen will. And, by consistently maintaining the distinction between the "earthly" and "heavenly" dimensions of this life (and between the will as a "natural gift" and its conversion as a "supernatural gift"), these remedies offer a Christian approach to good and evil in the recognizable framework of pagan writers, who from ancient times drew the distinction between the good (*bonum*) and the highest good (*summum bonum*) of human life.

Second, these remedies will place the Reformed view of the will more clearly within the medieval tradition, without compromising the distinctive Reformation teaching either on the bondage of the will or on salvation by grace alone. Third, these remedies will help to meet the traditional Catholic charge against Reformed theology, that it tends to neglect nature in the interest of promoting grace. Etienne Gilson once expressed this charge as follows: "St. Thomas never thought that to despise creation even for the purpose of exalting revelation was an homage pleasing to God."[1] It is by divine creation that human beings possess a rational-moral *nature* consisting of reason and will; by divine revelation and regeneration that God's grace restores to that nature the spiritual gifts of faith, hope, and love that it lost in the Fall. On that much, Catholic and Calvinist are agreed. It remains only for the Calvinist to revise Calvin's concept of the fallen will, and for the Catholic to revise the Thomist intellectualist view of the will, in order to unite them in a common Christian anthropology.

What are the implications of Calvin's voluntarism for Reformed epistemology? The short answer, implicit in my brief discussion in the Introduction, is that Reformed epistemologists who follow Plantinga's lead will need to develop a Reformed theory of the powers of the soul, not only of its noetic faculties (the senses as well as the intellect), but also of its volitional power (the will). The point of such a development is, of course, to explain the relationship between intellect and will in more detail than I have offered in this book, and more correctly than Reformed theologians or philosophers have done in the past. Three questions arise immediately. First, how did God intend these powers to function *properly* (to use Plantinga's term), that is, as he created them? Second, how do they now function, improperly, because of the fall? And third, how can they begin to function properly again upon a person's conversion to Christ? These three questions open up for Reformed thinkers a very large project indeed.

The Twin Engines of Reformed Epistemology [2]

I see two specific implications for Reformed epistemology that will be an important part of this large project. By way of review, first, let me note that Reformed epistemology makes two basic claims about our knowledge of God.[3] The first is its *immediacy*. Calvin formulates the idea in the very opening chapters of his *Institutes*: "There is within the human mind, and indeed by natural instinct an awareness of divinity," so deeply "inscribed in the hearts of all" that no one can blot it out. This "conviction, namely, that there is some God, is naturally inborn in all, and is fixed deep within, as it were in the very marrow." Indeed, this natural, direct knowledge of God is the "seed of religion," so that it is also the final explanation for the universality of religion among humankind, past and present (1.3.1–3).

The second Reformed claim about our knowledge of God is its *vitality*. By this term I refer to Calvin's claim that our knowledge of God is inevitably accompanied by a *religious* response. This response is of two quite opposite kinds. One is the response of piety: "Indeed, we shall not say that, properly speaking, God is known where there is no religion or piety" (1.2.1). By "piety" Calvin means "that reverence joined with the love of God which the knowledge of his benefits induces" (1.2.1). The alternate response is impiety, which consists in the lack of reverence for God, the failure to acknowledge him as the source of all life's benefits, and the corruption of religion by superstition and idolatry (1.1.2–3). This negative religious response includes a "degeneration from the true knowledge of God" and even an active effort to suppress it; the effort, however, never quite succeeds (1.4).

Alvin Plantinga has done more than anyone else to inject the first of these two claims from the Reformed theological tradition about our knowledge of God into the contemporary revival of religious epistemology. In his earlier writings, as I mentioned in the Introduction, Plantinga defends the Reformed teaching of *immediacy* by arguing that belief in God can be a "properly basic belief." By this term Plantinga means that belief in God (that is, belief *that God exists*) is as much in the "foundation" of human thought as the belief in the existence of other minds, the sensible world, and the self-evident truths of logic and mathematics.

In his later writings Plantinga argues that this foundational belief in God is produced in our minds when our noetic faculties are working properly in an environment suited for their proper functioning. So far, however, he has only mentioned in passing the second claim of the Reformed tradition, what I call the *vitality* of our knowledge of God, the claim that this knowledge is always accompanied by a religious response. This means also that he has not said very much about the effect of the will on reason's direct, immediate knowledge of God.

Plantinga first set forth his "Reformed epistemology" in a famous polemic entitled "The Reformed Objection to Natural Theology."[4] The focus of that paper upon natural theology is important in part because advocates of natural theology typically assume the adequacy of reason to demonstrate the existence of God pretty much *apart* from the religious condition of the will, *apart* from whether or not the natural theologian has any initial religious or irreligious response to the question of God's existence. Since the appearance of Plantinga's polemic, however, both Reformed epistemologists and their critics have neglected to explore the second ingredient of Calvin's teaching, what I call the vitality of our knowledge of God, the inevitability of a religious response that accompanies it. Nevertheless, Plantinga has explicitly acknowledged this ingredient from the beginning. Having discussed several quotations from the opening chapters in Calvin's *Institutes*, he sums up his objection to natural theology as follows:

> The Christian does not *need* natural theology, either as the source of his confidence or to justify his belief. Furthermore, the Christian *ought* not to believe on the basis of argument; if he does, his faith is likely to be "unstable and wavering," the "subject of perpetual doubt. . . ." From Calvin's point of view believing in the existence of your spouse on the basis of the analogical argument for other minds—whimsical at best and unlikely to delight the person concerned.[5]

In this summary we can distinguish *two* objections, which correspond to Calvin's two doctrines of the *immediacy* and *vitality* of our knowledge of God.

First, human beings *do not need* the inferential reasonings of natural theology for their belief in God to be justified, precisely because that belief can be "properly basic." Second, they *ought not* to believe in God on the basis of argument because it will then neither be a stable basis for their belief in God nor will it "delight" him. The latter reason why they ought not to believe in God on the basis of argument, that it would not delight God, suggests the religious condition I want to emphasize here. Since knowledge of God is direct and immediate, like our knowledge of our fellow human beings of whom we have direct experience, *arguing for* his existence will offend him. For it assumes there is something we know better (the premise of our argument, which may be some fact, say, about the world, like its amazing orderliness and design) than we know God himself (the conclusion from this premise, that he exists). But this is exactly not the way God made us, if Calvin is right in his claim that God gave us a natural disposition to develop a direct awareness of his presence, which is expressed in the belief that he exists. To be in the presence of another person, human or divine, requires an *acknowledgement* of that person. That presence not only makes argument for the person's existence unnecessary, it forbids our constructing an argument for that person's existence, since doing so would be an affront to the person in whose presence we are.

Now Plantinga's efforts in this paper, as in his other writings so far, are devoted almost entirely to establishing the plausibility of his first objection, that no one needs the inferential reasonings of natural theology to know that God exists. This is not the place to go into these arguments. I do want to emphasize, however, that Plantinga clearly refers also to the *religious* character of this direct and immediate knowledge of God. In addition to the passage just cited, he says: "Believing in God is indeed more than accepting the proposition that God exists." For the Christian, "belief in God means trusting God, accepting God, accepting his purposes, committing one's life to him and living in his presence." In this sense, "belief in God" is synonymous with religious "faith" and, as Plantinga notes, *that* must be carefully distinguished from "belief that God exists."[6]

Incidentally, the ambiguity of the phrase "belief in God," which is used to express both ideas (*belief that God exists* and *faith*), is critical to the entire discussion generated by the advocates of Reformed epistemology, for it has led to serious confusion, including Plantinga's own discussion.[7] The confusion is that the phrase "belief in God" often conceals the all-important difference between the Reformed claim, on the one hand, about the *natural immediacy* of our knowledge that God exists (as opposed to the *inferential* nature of that knowledge presupposed by natural theology) and, on the other, about the *religious response* that properly accompanies this knowledge.

The former is an *epistemic* claim about the belief *that* God exists, which is a propositional belief, an act of the intellect; it focuses on the *basis* of such a belief. The latter is a claim about belief *in* God, which, since it includes a trusting response to God, requires an act of the will. In the case of believers, this response is identified as *Christian faith*; in the case of those who lack this faith, the response is identified as *unbelief*. Each of these quite opposite responses, however, presupposes the direct and immediate knowledge that God exists. Indeed, this immediate knowledge of God is not a matter of faith at all; as Plantinga says, it is a "deliverance of reason" common to all mankind.[8] It is not, however, the result of *inferential* reason, since it is formed in the intellect by virtue of the *sensus divinitatis*, directly, immediately, foundationally, just like other properly basic beliefs.

Voluntarism and Revealed Beliefs

I can now outline the two important implications of Calvin's voluntarism for Reformed epistemology. The first implication concerns the nature of the *revealed beliefs* that believers accept by faith. Here it is necessary to take account of Plantinga's general claim about the involuntary nature of belief. This claim suggests, at first sight, that there is no role for the will, fallen or converted, to play in the formation or abandonment of belief. This suggestion would be mistaken, however, if indeed Calvin's voluntarism is as deep and pervasive as I have found it to be in this book.

So what is Plantinga's position on the voluntariness of belief? He writes: "If you order me now, for example, to cease believing that the earth is very old, there is no way I can comply with your order. But in the same way, it is not now within my power to cease believing in God now."[9] Now this involuntarist concept of belief seems to be strengthened by Plantinga's further claim for the belief that God exists, that it is a properly basic belief. For if any of our beliefs are involuntary, it would seem to be our foundational beliefs, such as belief in the external world, the existence of other minds, self-evident beliefs, beliefs about numbers and their relationships, and probably our elementary moral beliefs as well.

Now it is just this combination, in Plantinga's epistemology, of his general claim that our beliefs are involuntary with his specific claim that our belief that God exists is properly basic, that has occasioned what can be called the voluntarist objection to Reformed epistemology.

Surprising as it may seem at first, it has arisen among Catholic philosophers who are broadly influenced by the Thomistic, intellectualist tradition (which has also been home to natural theology since the thirteenth century). The objection has been developed recently by several authors in *Rational Faith*, Linda Zagzebski's collection of *Catholic Responses to Reformed Epistemology*, as the subtitle describes their work.[10]

The core of the objection, in Zagzebski's words, springs from "cognitive voluntarism," a view on which "Catholics have generally assigned a higher degree of voluntary control over belief and the processes leading to belief than have Protestants."[11] Unfortunately, in developing this objection, the contributors to her book generally fail to make the distinction between the two senses of "belief in God" that I insisted on earlier. As the title of Zagzebski's volume suggests, its authors[12] argue their objection to Reformed epistemology by discussing mainly the *revealed* beliefs of the Christian *faith* (the beliefs that only Christian theists accept), not the *natural* belief that God exists (that is, the generic theistic belief that Calvin says is innate in all human beings, which Plantinga calls a properly basic belief).

Now this defense by some Catholic philosophers of "cognitive voluntarism" as applied to revealed beliefs held by faith creates two problems, one for their own defense of natural theology and one for Plantinga's objection to it. The problem for the cognitive voluntarist is that Plantinga's original objection was not against the Catholic doctrine of *faith* but against *natural theology*, not only as espoused by Catholics but also (and especially, perhaps) as espoused by any kind of classical foundationalist who rests the rationality of religious belief on the success or failure of natural theology. So in focusing upon the revealed beliefs of faith rather than on natural theology, their voluntarist objection actually argues past the first point of Plantinga's objection to natural theology, that it is not needed for the justification of the belief that God exists.

On the other hand, their focus on revealed beliefs creates a problem for Plantinga. For, as I hinted earlier, Plantinga himself mingles the natural belief that God exists (on which the issue between Calvin's doctrine of the immediacy of Calvin's *sensus divinitatis* versus natural theology is joined) with revealed beliefs that only Christians accept, and accept only by faith. In the course of his defense of belief in God as properly basic, Plantinga offers, indiscriminately, examples of *both* kinds of belief, the belief that God exists *and* revealed beliefs. As examples of the latter he includes the belief "God is speaking to me" when I read the Bible and "God is to be thanked and praised"; indeed, he suggests that these beliefs are more likely to function as properly basic than "the relatively high-level and general proposition *God exists*" that these beliefs entail.[13]

If, however, as I suggested earlier, the proper basicality of a belief implies that it is involuntary, then to claim proper basicality for revealed beliefs implies that they are formed in the Christian believer as involuntarily as the natural belief that God exists is formed in all human beings. But that, in turn, implies that the faith on which acceptance of these revealed beliefs depends is likewise an involuntary mental state. But faith is a virtue and hence involves an act of will. It follows that the acceptance of revealed beliefs cannot be an involuntary matter comparable to the acceptance of the "deliverances of reason," or at least not in the same way that Plantinga claims for how the belief that God exists arises from the naturally implanted *sensus divinitatis*. In short, how can a revealed belief both arise in the properly basic way and yet depend on the act of will presupposed by the faith on which it depends? So far Plantinga has not addressed that problem. What Reformed epistemology requires, it seems, is a "free-will defense" of Christian faith, to head off the theological determinism implicit in the claim that revealed beliefs are involuntary, comparable to the "free-will defense" of moral action that Plantinga has mounted to head off the atheological objection to theism from the existence of evil.

This, then, is the first point at which the voluntarism of Calvin has an explicit bearing on Reformed epistemology. To summarize: Reformed epistemologists will have to agree with their Catholic voluntarist objectors that Christian faith, which includes an acceptance of the revealed beliefs dependent on it, involves the will in a way that a universal, generic belief that God exists does not. They may not accept the precise way Catholic authors (those, for example, whose views are represented in Zagzebski's volume) argue for the involvement of the will. Indeed, my guess is they would not, for they will question the extent to which these cognitive voluntarists still rely on evidentialism in addition to their invocation of the will. If this guess is correct, there is all the more reason that Reformed theologians and philosophers must develop a Reformed version of how the exercise of will is involved in the formation of faith and of revealed beliefs.

Before concluding this section, however, it should be noted that Plantinga has already significantly qualified his claim about the involuntary character of belief. He observes that there are culpable beliefs—racism, for example.[14] But a belief cannot be culpable if it is not in some way within our control. Racist beliefs are beliefs people voluntarily acquire, as Plantinga explains:

> Perhaps at some time in the past he [the racist] decided to accept these views. . . . To accept the view that such behavior is perfectly proper requires something like a special act of will—a special act of *ill* will. Such a person, we think, *knows better*, chooses what in some sense he knows to be wrong.[15]

But if there are culpable beliefs, why can't there also be praiseworthy beliefs, beliefs arising from choices of a good will? Clearly, Plantinga has at least opened the door to the role of the will and its influence on the intellect.

And he has opened it more than just a crack. He discusses the example of a Christian who doubts one of his revealed beliefs, that God was in Christ reconciling the world to himself. "Upon calling that belief to mind, he finds it cold, lifeless, without warmth or attractiveness. Nonetheless he is committed to this belief; it is his position; if you ask him what he thinks about it, he will unhesitatingly endorse it."[16] What is going on here? Says Plantinga:

> Let us say that he *accepts* this proposition, even though when he is assailed by doubt, he may fail to *believe* it—at any rate explicitly—to an appreciable degree. His commitment to this proposition may be much stronger than his explicit and occurrent belief in it; so these two—that is acceptance and belief—must be distinguished.[17]

Even revealed beliefs, of course, must be formulated and understood (at some level) by the intellect, but if their *acceptance* is a matter of commitment, what is this but an admission that one's beliefs are in that respect subject to the will?

Indeed, if the degree of acceptance of one's beliefs is a matter of the will, why doesn't how one acquires a particular belief in the first place, or abandons it later for a contrary belief, also depend on the will? Again, it seems clear that Plantinga opens up, perhaps even espouses, a voluntarist conception of belief that radically qualifies his other claims about our not being able to change our beliefs. But his voluntarist objectors have failed to notice.

Moreover, in elaborating on the distinction between acceptance and belief, Plantinga asserts that

> . . . while we may perhaps agree that what I believe is not *directly* within my control, some of my beliefs are indirectly within my control, at least in part. First, what I accept has a long-term influence upon what I believe. . . . Although it is not within my power now to cease believing now, there may be a series of action, such that I can now take the first and, after taking the first, will be able to take the second, and so on; and after taking the whole series of actions I will no longer believe in God.[18]

Now it isn't entirely clear which type of belief, the natural belief that God exists or revealed beliefs, Plantinga has in mind here. His reference to Pascal's advice suggests the latter; but these (revealed beliefs) more clearly involve the will than the former.

No matter, however; the point is that Plantinga is dealing, in an eminently Calvinist way, with some version of a voluntarist concept of the will's relationship to the intellect.

Even if Reformed epistemology can acknowledge the voluntary character of revealed beliefs, however, the question remains, how can this recognition be squared with Plantinga's suggestion that revealed beliefs, as well as the belief that God exists, are *properly basic*? His suggestion, considered quite apart from the voluntarist question, seems plausible enough. If, for example, I believe that God is speaking to me when I am reading the Bible (or hear it read), Calvin would say that I do so on the inner testimony of the Holy Spirit. If so, that (revealed) belief, or any other revealed belief to which it gives rise—say that "God loves me and the whole world also"—seems to be as directly and immediately known to me as the belief that God exists is known to anyone in virtue of the universally implanted sense of divinity.

This further question also suggests, incidentally, that the Reformed epistemologist's concept of properly basic beliefs plays a significantly larger role than just as the basis for an objection to natural theology. For the concept of properly basic beliefs may also account in some way for beliefs acquired by way of the testimony of other persons, human or divine (the latter as in the preceding paragraph), in addition to those acquired by one's own observation and experience. But it will have to account for these testimonial beliefs in a way that is compatible with their sometimes being voluntary beliefs, rooted in faith. And faith, of course, is not limited to divine faith (belief in God); it includes human faith, the faith we have in our fellow human beings, by which we accept their testimony for a great many things we claim to know.[19]

Voluntarism and the Belief that God Exists

We must now outline the second implication of Calvin's voluntarism for Reformed epistemology, which concerns the universal natural belief that God exists. For that belief, on the Calvinist view, seems not to be a voluntary belief at all, but a belief that all human beings form *naturally* in the course of their growing up within the universal conditions of human experience in virtue of their inborn sense of divinity. Still, there is a Calvinist claim that rings with voluntarism even with respect to this belief, for which there seems to be no parallel in the Catholic voluntarist approach to religious belief.

As I noted earlier, if any beliefs are involuntary, it would seem to be our foundational beliefs as they have traditionally been conceived. If the belief that God exists is properly basic, then, it shares with these other properly basic beliefs (like the belief in the external world, the belief in other minds, and self-evident beliefs) an important characteristic typical of such foundational beliefs, namely, that they are normally more directly known and certain for us, beyond our ability easily to doubt them, than many other beliefs that are inferentially based upon them. So what is the peculiar role of will that the Calvinist proposes with respect to the foundational belief that God exists?

It is the claim that we can and do *resist* this belief, in such a way that we form other beliefs that are culpable beliefs, for example, that maybe God doesn't exist. Even though we do not originally form the belief that God exists by an act of will, we can, as an act of will, suppress it. If the result of such suppression is a culpable belief, however, not only must *this* belief be willful, it must also be formed in the presence of better knowledge, as Plantinga explains in the case of racist beliefs. Now the unique feature of Reformed epistemology is that it provides an account of just what this better knowledge consists of, in the face of which the contrary beliefs are formed. This better knowledge consists of the direct, original, foundational acquaintance with God himself. And this acquaintance includes, for Calvin at least, not only the bare belief that God exists, but also the beliefs that he is our Maker, that he is just one God, and that he is majestic and ought, therefore, to be worshiped (1.2.1; 1.10.3).

The first advantage of this account of our *better knowledge of God* is obvious: it escapes the objection of the cognitive voluntarists. For if the formation of the belief that God exists is originally not a matter of the will at all, the voluntarist objection, which assumes that we have control over the formation of some of our beliefs, is irrelevant insofar as it is aimed at this belief, no matter how correct it may be with respect to revealed beliefs.

The second advantage is less obvious but more important. In providing the necessary basis for the culpability of questioning the existence of God, Reformed epistemology provides an account of an essential teaching of Scripture, for which Paul's claim in Romans 1:18–21 has become the *locus classicus* of support. God has made himself known to all human beings in such a way that they are without excuse for suppressing such knowledge, let alone for not honoring him or giving him thanks. According to this teaching, it is an original responsibility human beings possess: to acknowledge something they cannot really help believing, namely, that God exists.

On the voluntarist objection, by contrast, our first responsibility is to seek a *rational justification* for the belief that God exists. Typically, the writers who develop this objection hold that such a justification lies in a combination of evidence and faith. Patrick Lee,[20] for example, puts it this way:

> The main functions of evidence or reasons in religious belief is not to show the truth of what is believed—for then *faith* would not be required. Nor is the main function of reasons even to show the truth of the factual proposition that God has spoken. Rather, the main function of reasons in religious belief is to show the truth of the moral proposition that I ought to believe.[21]

So cognitive voluntarism is not pure voluntarism, but a voluntarism based on, or at least combined with, some form of evidentialism.

But suppose (on Lee's approach) we have found some appropriate evidence that supports an obligation to believe in God. What if that evidence is still insufficient to motivate us to fulfill the obligation? In that case, it appears, we will have no responsibility to acknowledge, honor, and thank him for our lives and his gifts. Our failure to reach an adequate rational justification for the obligation to believe will have undercut what the Bible teaches is an original (in the sense of primitive, underived) responsibility, namely, to acknowledge the God who made us and claims the original authority over our lives.

The Reformed view, however, can account for this original responsibility, for it teaches that the belief that God exists (and is our Creator and supreme benefactor) must be essentially a matter beyond our control; it constitutes a knowledge we cannot escape, no matter how hard we try. That is the import of Calvin's teaching and of its adumbration in Plantinga's claim that belief that God exists is a properly basic belief, and thus an involuntary belief. As such, this belief directly obliges us to recognize God, rather than its being the case that we are first obliged by some reasoning and evidence to have this belief.

Of course, as we saw earlier in our discussion of revealed beliefs, Reformed epistemologists will need to work out some account by which to distinguish properly basic beliefs that are involuntary from those that are not.

There has to be a reason why the natural belief that God exists is *not* a matter of faith in the way that the acceptance of revealed beliefs *is*.

The Twin Engines Run Together

We can finally see the bearing of the Reformed thesis about the immediacy of our knowledge of God on what I have called its vitality. The immediacy of our knowledge of God is precisely what creates this vitality, namely, our religious obligation to him, which is an original obligation of our lives. This original obligation cannot be undercut by any prior epistemic responsibility to acquire evidence, either that God exists or that we have an obligation to believe that he does. Hence, the belief that God exists cannot be a volitional belief, a matter of faith, to obtain which is "up to us." Of course, we may try to ignore, resist, suppress, or reject this belief, and in that sense the belief is not beyond the reach of our will. But any such effort of the will can neither be rational (in accord with the proper function of our reason) nor religiously correct, any more than can any other sin.

So there is a close connection between the two Reformed objections to natural theology, that it isn't necessary to base our belief in God on evidence and that it would not even be appropriate to try. If (resorting to Plantinga's analogy) it is unnecessary to establish inferentially the existence of one's wife in her presence, it is also morally inappropriate. For given who she is, a fellow human being, and, moreover, one in a special relationship to her husband, she would be offended by such an effort on his part. A fortiori, God, given who he is (our Creator and ultimate benefactor, in whose very presence we live, move, and have our being), will be far more offended by a similar effort.

Two implications of Calvin's voluntaristic view of the will for Reformed epistemology should now be evident, one for the account it must give of revealed beliefs as beliefs accepted by faith, one for the possibility of resisting the involuntary, foundational belief that God exists. If revealed beliefs are properly basic, it must be shown how they can still depend upon an act of will, as they must if they depend upon faith. And if the belief that God exists is an involuntary belief, it must be shown in detail how it is formed in us, without an act of will but as a deliverance of reason itself, in spite of the fact that it is subject to willful resistance and neglect.

Conclusion

The development of Reformed epistemology has just begun. I hope it includes a thorough reexamination of traditional Reformed teaching on the relationship between will and intellect as they were created, on the persistence of this relationship in its fallen state, and on what it means for this relationship to be restored in the divine process of human redemption.

Soli deo gloria, deo naturae et gratiae.

Notes

Introduction

1. John Calvin, *Institutes of the Christian Religion*, 2 vols., translated by F. L. Battles (Philadelphia: Westminster, 1960), 1.15.8. Citations from this work hereafter will be located in the text, not in the notes.

2. Plantinga first uses the term "Reformed epistemology" in "The Reformed Objection to Natural Theology," *Proceedings of the American Catholic Philosophical Association* (1980). For the first phase to which I refer, see "Reason and Belief in God," *Faith and Rationality: Reason and Belief in God,* ed. A. Plantinga and N. Wolterstorff (Grand Rapids: Eerdmans, 1983). For the second phase, see Alvin Plantinga, *Warrant and Proper Function* (New York: Oxford University Press, 1993).

3. Thomas F. Torrance, *Calvin's Doctrine of Man* (Grand Rapids: Eerdmans, 1957), 7.

4 Ibid., 8.

5. T. H. L. Parker, *Calvin's Doctrine of the Knowledge of God* (Grand Rapids: Eerdmans, 1959), 3.

6. Mary Potter Engel, *John Calvin's Perspectival Anthropology* (Atlanta: Scholars Press, 1988), xif, chapter 1.

7. Ibid., 4.

8. Ibid., 53–54.

9. Ibid., 193.

10. Ibid., 189ff.

11. John H. Leith, "The Doctrine of the Will in the Institutes of the Christian Religion," *Reformation Perennis*, ed. B. A. Gerrish and R. Benedetto (Pittsburgh: The Pickwick Press, 1981), 49–66.

12. A. N. S. Lane, "Did Calvin Believe in Free Will?" *Vox Evangelica* 12 (1981), 72–90.

13. Leith, "Doctrine of the Will," 49.

14. Ibid., 62.

15. Lane, "Did Calvin believe in Free Will?" 86.

16. R. T. Kendall, *Calvin and English Calvinism to 1649* (New York and London: Oxford University Press, 1978). For a critical account of Kendall, see Paul Helm, *Calvin and the Calvinists* (Edinburgh: The Banner of Truth Trust, 1981).

17. Richard A. Muller, "Fides and Cognitio in Relation to the Problem of Intellect and Will in the Theology of John Calvin," *Calvin Theological Journal,* vol. 25 (Nov. 1990), 207–224. See also his later "Grace, Election, and Contingent Choice: Arminius's Gambit and the Reformed Response," *The Grace of God, the Bondage of the Will,* vol. 2, ed. T. R. Schreiner and B. A. Ware (Grand Rapids:

Baker Books, 1995), 251–278. The main focus of this later article is on free will and election, but in one section Muller shows that Calvin and later Reformed thinkers typically understand by "free will" the will's being "free from external constraint" (what I call its minimalist sense in chapter 1 below), not "free to make contrary choices," especially with regard to salvation (269–277).

18. Muller, "Fides and Cognitio," 211.

19. Ibid., 223.

20. Ibid., 223.

21. Ibid., 223.

22. Ibid., 214, n. 27.

Chapter 1

1. For the complexity of the biblical concept of "heart," see John Cooper, *Body, Soul, and Life Everlasting* (Grand Rapids: Eerdmans, 1989), 45–47, 107. For Calvin's tendency to use the term synonymously with "will" see *Institutes* 2.2.27; 2.3.6–10. For an extensive account of the development of the biblical idea of "will," see Albrecht Dihle, *The Theory of Will in Classical Antiquity* (Berkeley: University of California Press, 1982), especially chapters 4–6.

2. Alan Donagan, "Thomas Aquinas on Human Action," *The Cambridge History of Later Medieval Philosophy*, ed. N. Kretzmann, A. Kenny, and J. Pinboorg (Cambridge: Cambridge University Press, 1982), 642–54. Donagan's essay includes additional distinctions St. Thomas makes, as do the other commentators on Aquinas and Scotus cited below. They are not necessary for the points I will be making later about Calvin's view of the will.

3. The most difficult situations to explain on this account are cases of weakness of will and sin (of which more, later). The two concepts raise similar problems. An extensive philosophical literature on weakness of will (Gr. *akrasia*) has appeared in the last few decades, which is well worth the attention of Christian philosophers and theologians who write on sin and on the fall.

4. So called by contemporary philosophers of mind and action theory after Thomas Reid (1710–1796). We shall return to the concept in chapter 3, note 13.

5. Plato's articulation of these topics is more complex than this brief summary suggests. For a standard account, see G. M. A. Grube, *Plato's Thought* (Indianapolis: Hackett Publishing Co., 1980), chapters III "Eros," IV "The Nature of the Soul," and VII, i "Virtue and Knowledge." The close association of soul (the principle of life), *eros* (the motive of love), and reason (the power to know) can be traced in A. E. Taylor, *Plato: The Man and His Work* (New York: World Publishing Co., 1964), 223ff; 226; 230ff; 306ff; 491.

6. See W. D. Ross, *Aristotle* (New York: Meridian, 1960), chapters 5 "Psychology" and 7 "Ethics"; J. L. Ackrill, *Aristotle the Philosopher* (Oxford: Oxford University Press, 1984), chapter 10 "Ethics."

7. Whether Aristotle agrees with Plato on this issue has been much disputed. I believe that what Aristotle says in *Nicomachean Ethics*, trans. Martin Ostwald (Indianapolis: Bobbs–Merrill, 1962) 1146a 5ff and 1147b 15–17 offers decisive support for such agreement. See Jon Moline, *Plato's Theory of Understanding* (Madison: University of Wisconsin Press, 1981), 26–27; R. M. Hare, *Plato* (New York: Oxford University Press, 1982), chapter 8; and J. J. Walsh, *Aristotle's Con-*

ception of Moral Weakness (New York: Columbia University Press, 1963), chapter 4.

8. Eleonore Stump, "Intellect, Will, and the Principle of Alternative Possibilities," *Christian Theism and the Problems of Philosophy,* ed. Michael Beaty (Notre Dame: University of Notre Dame Press, 1990), 269.

9. Donagan, "Thomas Aquinas," 644.

10. Thomas Aquinas, *Summa Theologica, Basic Writings of Saint Thomas Aquinas,* 2 vols., ed. A. C. Pegis (New York: Random House, 1945), 1, 82, 3 ad 2. All references to the *Summa Theologica* below are to this edition except where noted otherwise.

Aquinas qualifies this primacy of the intellect in the next Article of Question 82. After making a distinction to allow for the primacy of the will as well as the primacy of the intellect, he concludes: "From this we can easily understand why these powers include one another in their acts, because the intellect understands that the will wills, and the will wills the intellect to understand" (1, 82, 4, ad 1). The wording of this conclusion might suggest only the "complicated feedback system" that Stump sees in Aquinas's account (see note 8 above and 16 below). But Aquinas presently reaffirms the primacy of the intellect in the relevant sense: "Every movement of the will must be preceded by apprehension, whereas every apprehension is not preceded by an act of the will" (1, 82, 4, ad 2).

As will become evident below, however, Aquinas must forsake this simple primacy of the intellect in order to account for sin (see note 19).

11. For a contemporary account of these two concepts of freedom, see Anthony Kenny, *Will, Freedom, and Power* (New York: Harper and Row, 1975).

12. Aquinas, *Summa Theologica,* 1, 82, 2, ad 1. See also 1–2, 13, 6, ad 3.

13. Donagan, "Thomas Aquinas," 652f.

14. Stump, "Intellect," 267. Aquinas says: "The act of the reason can always be commanded, as when one is told to be attentive, and to use one's reason" (1–2, 17, 6, *Respondeo*).

15. Ibid., 268.

16. Ibid., 270.

17. Aquinas, *Summa Theologica,* translated by the Fathers of the English Dominican Province, vol. 13 (London: Oates and Washbourne, 1932), 2–2, 163, 2.

18. Aquinas, *Basic Writings,* 1–2, 74, 1, ad 1.

19. Ibid., 1–2, 74, 1; 2. (See note 10 above).

20. Ibid., 1–2, 74, 5.

21. Ibid., 1–2, 83, 3. But Aquinas manifests the same inconsistency we shall find in Calvin in chapter 2. Two Questions later he implies that reason was created with a "perfect hold over the lower parts of the soul," having in the present Question attributed original sin to a will that did *not* submit to that hold of reason over it (1–2, 85, 3, *Respondeo*).

22. Quoted by Patrick Lee, "The Relation Between Intellect and Will in Free Choice According to Aquinas and Scotus," *The Thomist,* vol. 49 (July 1985), 322.

23. Ibid., 322ff.

24. Vernon J. Bourke entitles his chapter on voluntarism "Freedom as the Genus of Volition" (chapter 4) in *Will in Western Thought* (New York: Sheed and Ward, 1964). He discusses the Bible, Augustine, Anselm, Bernard, Scotus, Ockham, and Descartes under this category.

25. Alan Wolter notes that, although Scotus says that the human will "mirrors in some fashion what God possesses pure and simply," he does not pursue the analogy between the creative character of our will and God's. *The Philosophical Theology of John Duns Scotus,* ed. Marilyn Adams (Ithaca: Cornell University Press, 1990), 176ff.

26. Bernardine Bonansea, *Man and His Approach to God in John Duns Scotus* (Lanham, Md.: University Press of America, 1983), 56.

27. As Bonansea points out, 56, n. 20, Scotus's reference to Augustine, *Retractations* 1.22 seems mistaken. The sentence is found, among other places, in *On the Free Choice of the Will* 3.3.7.

28 Mark Pestana, "Radical Freedom, Radical Evil and the Possibility of Eternal Damnation," *Faith and Philosophy* 9 (October 1992), 500–508.

29. Ibid., 505.

30. Shakespeare, *Julius Caesar,* act 2, scene 2. On the irrationality of evil doing, compare what Donald Davidson says at the end of his well-known article, "How Is Weakness of the Will Possible?" "What is special in incontinence is that the actor cannot understand himself: he recognizes, in his own intentional behaviour, something essentially surd." *Essays on Actions and Events* (Oxford: Clarendon Press, 1980), 42.

31. Lee, "Relation Between Intellect and Will," 341.

32. Ibid., 341.

33. As was Augustine, much earlier, in his account of his theft of the pears; see *Confessions* (Garden City, N.Y.: Doubleday, 1960), Book 2.

34. Bonansea, *Man and His Approach,* 79. See also 57, n. 25.

35. Wolter, *Philosophical Theology,* 106.

36. Bonansea, *Man and His Approach,* 79.

37. A very extensive (and vivid) contemporary exploration of the "mystery of iniquity" is by Cornelius Plantinga, *Not the Way It's Supposed to Be* (Grand Rapids: Eerdmans, 1995). See especially chapter 7, "Sin and Folly."

38. Anthony Kenny, "Descartes on the Will," *The Anatomy of the Soul* (New York: Harper and Row, 1973), 112. Kenny argues against those who claim to detect a late development in Descartes, from intellectualism to voluntarism, by showing that the voluntaristic strain is present already in his earlier works. See also Kenny's previous study, *Descartes: A Study of His Philosophy* (New York: Random House, 1968), 70; 173–74. For Descartes's account of the absolute freedom of God ("Universal Possibilism"), see Alvin Plantinga, *Does God Have a Nature?* (Milwaukee: Marquette University Press, 1980), 92–126.

39. Quoted by Kenny from Descartes's "Geometrical Exposition," following his "Objections, II" (AT VII 166; HR II 56), Kenny, "Descartes on the Will," 82 (emphasis mine).

40. Rene Descartes, "Meditations" 4, *Discourse on Method and Meditations* (Indianapolis: Hackett, 1980). Anthony Kenny cites the same passage in support of the point, Kenny, "Descartes on the Will," 98ff.

41. Quoted by Kenny from Descartes' letter to Mesland (1645) (AT VI, 197), cited in its entirety by Kenny, "Descartes on the Will," 107.

42. The qualification "clearly perceived" is important, for the tradition had long distinguished the intellect's involuntary assent to such a truth from its voluntary assent to the truth of the articles of *faith*, i.e., of propositions that are not "clearly perceived" to be true by the natural light of reason. Thus Augustine had written, "Faith is thinking with assent" (*Predestination of the Saints*, 5) and Aquinas had added: "when the intellect is moved by the will" (*S. T.* 2–2, 2, 2 *Respondeo*).

43. See Descartes's remarkable reminiscence on his project in the *Meditations* in the later *Principles of Philosophy*, in *The Philosophical Works of Descartes*, trans. E. S. Haldane & G. R. T. Ross (New York: Dover, 1931), Part I, 39.

44. Ibid., Part I, 32 (emphasis mine); see also 34.

45. The will's unlimited freedom is not a defect in the will but a sign of its perfection: "I observe it to be so great in me that I grasp an idea of nothing greater, to the extent that the will is principally the basis for my understanding that I bear an image and likeness of God" (*Meditations*, 4; see also *The Passions of the Soul*, in Haldane and Ross, Part I, 41, 50).

46. Descartes, *Principles*, Part I, 37 (emphasis mine).

47. See Herman Dooyeweerd, *Transcendental Problems of Philosophic Thought* (Grand Rapids: Eerdmans, 1948), 59–77; *In the Twilight of Western Thought* (Philadelphia: Presbyterian and Reformed Publishing Co., 1960), 29–61.

Chapter 2

1. The long section between the last two sections, consisting of twelve chapters, 195 pages (2.6–17), elaborates on how Jesus Christ brings us from our fallen to our redeemed state.

2. Calvin's summary of Aristotle is misleading. It is not that the mind "is moved by choice" but that choice, which is the source of action, is motivated not by thought or reason alone, but by thought and desire working together. Says Aristotle: "The starting point of choice, however, is desire and reasoning directed toward some end." It is here that Aristotle lays the foundation for the concept of will as rational appetite: "Therefore, choice is either intelligence motivated by desire or desire operating through thought, and it is as a combination of these two that man is a starting point of action" (*Nicomachean Ethics* 1139b 4–5).

3. Lane smoothes over the inconsistency between Calvin's intellectualist account of the created state and his voluntaristic account of the fall by commenting on Calvin's phrase that the will is "perfectly submissive to the authority of reason" as follows: "This would imply that the will would inevitably obey reason, but this is not what Calvin meant" (Lane, "Did Calvin Believe in Free Will?" 73).

4. I am grateful to Richard Muller for encouraging me to read Francis Turretin (1623–1687) to get a sense of the precision with which Reformed theology was articulated within a century after his time. It is fascinating to watch Turretin attempt to avoid the inconsistency bequeathed him by his mentor. Although Turretin writes with clearer logic and less rhetoric, his effort is in vain. Like Calvin, he begins with an intellectualist account of the created will: "The liberty

of Adam . . . was not the liberty of a will undetermined by the practical intellect; for this would have changed the will into an irrational appetite, so that he would have sought evil as evil. This would not have been so much liberty as an unbridled license, incompatible (*asystatos*) with the image of God" (*Institutes of Elenctic Theology*, vol. 1, trans. G. M. Giger, ed. J. T. Dennison, Jr., Phillipsburg, N.J.: Presbyterian and Reformed Publishing Company, 1992, 8.1.6).

Turretin is careful to define Adam's "essential liberty" as consisting in "two characteristics: preference (*proairetikon*) and will (*to hekousion*), so that what is done may be done by a previous judgment of the reason and spontaneously" (8.1.6; see also 10.2.5 and 10.3.10, where he does the same for the fallen state). Thus Turretin absorbs *choice* ("preference") into the judgment of reason, in such a way that it is determined by that judgment rather than exercised by the will as a power of contrary choice.

How then did Adam fall? Not by choice thus absorbed into intellectual judgment, which defined Adam's liberty, but by the overall "mutability" of his nature (8.1.7–8). Introducing this term to explain the fall, while studiously avoiding the term "choice" as a component of the will, seems like a subterfuge to avoid locating the fall in a contrary choice of the will (*posse peccare et non peccare*). Indeed, Turretin actually restricts the latter sense of choice to the state of grace under which sinful believers live in this life, ascribing to Adam only the "power of not sinning" (*posse non peccare*) (8.1.9). But the question leaps from the page, how could Adam have had such power without its entailing also the contrary power of sinning? (see also 9.7.4–7). Turretin's answer: an insistence that freedom of the will can be reduced to its minimalist sense of spontaneity (9.7.8).

For further elaborations of the ambiguity, see 9.5 (on the fall of the angels) and 9.6 (on the fall of Adam).

5. Paul Helm, *Calvin and the Calvinists* (Edinburgh: The Banner of Truth Trust, 1981), 56.

6. See chapter 1, n. 8.

7. Muller, "Fides and Cognitio," 223.

8. Arvin Vos makes a convincing case that Calvin's and Aquinas's conceptions of faith are far closer to each other than is widely perceived, both by Calvinists and Thomists. Though he stops short of calling Calvin a voluntarist, he doesn't call Aquinas an intellectualist either! *Aquinas, Calvin, and Contemporary Protestant Thought* (Washington D.C. and Grand Rapids: Christian University Press and Eerdmans Publishing Co., 1985), chapter 1.

9. A very interesting passage is the following: "But how can the mind be aroused to taste the divine goodness without at the same time being wholly kindled to love God in return? For truly, that abundant sweetness which God has stored up for those who fear him cannot be known without at the same time powerfully moving us. And once anyone has been moved by it, it utterly ravishes him and draws him to itself" (3.2.41).

The passage is reminiscent of Plato and suggests his "internalist" approach, on which knowing the Good is sufficient to motivate the correct moral response. And indeed, Calvin is deeply influenced by Plato. But where Plato absorbs the motivation of *eros* into his concept of *nous*, by Calvin's time theologians had distinguished the will and the intellect as two different powers for the source of motivation and knowledge respectively. So does Calvin, as we have seen.

For a further discussion of this passage in Calvin and the issues of virtue and motivation it raises, see my *Happiness: Goal or Gift?—Two Lectures on the Relationship Between Knowledge, Goodness, and Happiness in Plato and Calvin. The Stob Lectures* (Grand Rapids: Calvin College, 1993–1994), 44–48. There I suggest that the relationship between will and intellect as changed by grace involves a deep paradox. In any event, Calvin's very next sentence ought to remove any doubt that the will is still at the heart (!) of his view of faith and conversion: "Therefore, it is no wonder if a perverse and wicked heart never experiences that emotion by which, borne up to heaven itself, we are admitted to the most hidden treasures of God and to the most hallowed precinct of his Kingdom, which should not be defiled by the entrance of an impure heart" (3.2.41).

10. See, for examples, Merold Westphal, "Taking Sin Seriously: Sin as an Epistemological Category," *Christian Philosophy,* ed. Thomas Flint (Notre Dame, Ind.: University of Notre Dame Press, 1990) and George Mavrodes, "A Futile Search for Sin," *Perspectives* 8 (January 1993), 9.

11. I present a more complete account of Calvin's ambivalence toward philosophy and his disapproval of speculation in *Faith and Reason From Plato to Plantinga* (Albany: State University of New York Press, 1881), 171ff.

12. Some contemporary Christian philosophers dispute this possibility. Alvin Plantinga, for one, writes, in his well-known "The Free Will Defense": "Now God can create free creatures, but He can't *cause* or *determine* them to do only what is right. For if He does so, then they aren't significantly free after all; they do not do what is right freely. To create creatures capable of *moral good,* therefore, He must create creatures capable of moral evil; and he can't give these creatures the freedom to perform evil and at the same time prevent them from doing so." (*God, Freedom, and Evil* [New York: Harper Torchbooks, 1974] 30. See also *God and Other Minds* [Ithaca: Cornell University Press, 1967], 132 and *The Nature of Necessity* [Oxford: The Clarendon Press, 1974], 165ff.).

13. Unless, as Turretin teaches, God at some point "withheld" this grace, which would have been "efficacious" in preventing the fall, thus making the fall possible (though not necessary, since Adam's "natural power of not sinning" gave him "strength sufficient to stand if he wished") (9.7.7). I have not been able to find a similar teaching in Calvin.

Chapter 3

1. This treatise, which has recently been translated into English for the first time, mainly reiterates Calvin's view of the will in the *Institutes,* with one important exception (see n. 13 below). See John Calvin, *The Bondage and Liberation of the Will: A Defense of the Orthodox Doctrine of Human Choice against Pighius,* ed. A. N. S. Lane and trans. G. I. Davies (Grand Rapids: Baker Books, 1996). I refer here and elsewhere to this document as Calvin's *Reply to Pighius,* as it commonly known.

2. It is evident from Calvin's many appeals to Augustine in support of his own doctrine of the fallen will that its seeds were firmly planted already by the great Latin Father. It is also evident that Augustine said enough about the survival of

the will and its natural powers after the fall to warrant the medieval appeal to him for the "principle" we are about to elaborate. These two facts suggest that Augustine's thought harbors the same inconsistency about the will that I purport to find in Calvin, so that it would be as important to point out the inconsistency in Augustine as in Calvin; but that rather sizeable project I leave to one side.

3 As we saw in chapter 2, before the fall, according to Calvin, these gifts were also dependent on grace—no difference there. The major difference is that prelapsarian grace, though necessary and sufficient for persistence in perfect goodness, was also resistible; whereas after the fall, while still necessary and sufficient, it is *irresistible*, which the Reformers identify as its effectualness or effectiveness. In either case, however, grace is a necessary condition, not for the *existence* of the natural powers of intellect and will themselves (with their components), since their existence in us is from divine creation; rather, grace is the necessary condition for certain *special exercises* of these natural powers, exercises like "faith and righteousness."

4. There is a conceptual oddity regarding the claim that our very nature is a gift. To be a gift implies not only a giver (God) but a receiver. But we did not exist before we were created with the nature we now have, so how can our nature be a gift to us? The oddity has not gone unnoticed. For example, Lewis Smedes writes: "It is strange even to think of our lives as a gift to ourselves. But anyone who has deeply felt dependence on God knows that, while paradoxical, it is not nonsense: every person's life is God's gift to himself or herself." See *Mere Morality* (Grand Rapids: Eerdmans, 1982), 109.

5. The dispute centers on the relationship of the supernatural gifts to the natural powers. Are these gifts "added on" to an already essentially complete human nature or are they integral to that essence? The answer, as I hope to show, is both. They are added on to the other exercises of intellect and will in such a way that they can be lost; but their presence or absence is integral, respectively, to the soundness or corruption of these other exercises.

6. This is an important point at which to recall Calvin's description of the will as it was created, which was discussed earlier in chapter 2. There we saw that the created will includes both inclination and choice.

7. Note 7 to 1.1.2 at the beginning of the Battles edition of the *Institutes* clarifies the point about the term "nature." There seems to be only one other explicit reference in the *Institutes* to the Manichean heresy directly connected with our topic (1.14.3), but the *Reply to Pighius* has many more, since Pighius had charged Calvin with Manicheanism (cf. especially 2.264; 3.295; 4.331; 5:361).

8. Calvin's followers are subject to the same slippage of sense. For example, Louis Berkhof in his *Systematic Theology* says of "total depravity," a term that harbors a similar ambiguity, that it was "the immediate concomitant of the first sin. . . . The contagion of his sin at once spread through the entire man, leaving no part of his nature untouched, but vitiating every power and faculty of body and soul" (*Systematic Theology* [Grand Rapids: Eerdmans, 1949], 225–26). But a few pages later, describing the essence of sin, Berkhof refers to its "absolute character": "There are no gradations between the good and the evil. The transition from the one to the other is not of a quantitative, but of a qualitative character. A moral being that is good does not become evil by simply diminishing

his goodness, but only by a radical qualitative change, by turning to sin. Sin is not a lesser degree of goodness, but a positive evil" (231–32). The second description suggests something more than the vitiation of every part of our nature, rather like every part is wholly vitiated, with no inherent goodness left.

In contrast, Aquinas carefully distinguishes between the "good of nature" and its being "diminished by sin": "The good of nature that is diminished by sin is the natural inclination to virtue, which is befitting to man from the very fact that he is a rational being; for it is due to this that he performs actions in accord with reason, which is to act virtuously. Now sin cannot entirely take away from man the fact that he is a rational being, for then he would no longer be capable of sin. Therefore it is not possible for this good of nature to be entirely destroyed" (Aquinas, *Basic Writings*, 1–2, 85, 2 *Respondeo*).

9. Later on I will comment on the important term "truly good" that Calvin uses here.

10. If this analysis seems unfair, consider what Calvin himself says next: "That no reader may remain in doubt, we must be warned of a double misinterpretation. For 'appetite' here signifies not an impulse of the will itself but rather an inclination of nature; and 'good' refers not to virtue or justice but to condition, as when things go well with man. To sum up, much as man desires to follow what is good, still he does not follow it. There is no man to whom eternal blessedness is not pleasing, yet no man aspires to it except by the impulsion of the Holy Spirit. The desire for well-being natural to men no more proves freedom of the will than the tendency of metals and stones toward perfection of their essence proves it in them" (2.2.26).

11. This interpretation has been disputed, even by Reformed commentators. Needless to say, the latter will be unable to appeal to Calvin's view of the fallen will to support their interpretation.

12. Lane, "Did Calvin Believe in Free Will?" 72.

13. Calvin's reaction to the concept here in the *Institutes* is quite different from that in his *Reply to Pighius*, where he actually invokes the concept himself to defend the responsibility of the fallen will: "Therefore we describe [as coerced] the will which does not incline this way or that of its own accord or by an internal movement of decision, but is forcibly driven by an external impulse. We say that it is *self-determined* when of itself it directs itself in the direction in which it is led, when it is not taken by force or dragged unwillingly. . . . Now you see how self-determination and necessity can be combined together" (2.280).

Unlike in the *Institutes*, Calvin here has no complaint about the presumptuousness that might accompany a claim to the self-determination of the will; rather, he insists on the claim to assure the the responsibility for bondage of sin in the face of its constituting a kind of necessity. The necessity that characterizes the self-determination of the will is different from the necessity created by its being externally compelled: the former is compatible with its freedom, the latter not.

The concept of self-determination is picked up by contemporary philosophers of mind in the term "agent causation," following Thomas Reid.

14. Leith, for example, tries to rescue Calvin in just this way. He writes: "While Calvin speaks of the loss of freedom of will in the sense of contrary

choice, a close reading indicates that he only denies freedom of the will as the power of choice in certain particular situations in which the self is deeply involved and in particular in the self's relationship to God. The freedom of the self resided both in the understanding and the will, and some measure of this freedom of choice remains to fallen man" ("Doctrine of the Will," 53).

Leith offers no textual support for this last claim; as I have shown, the textual support is prevailingly against it.

15. This is as good a point as any to reiterate my criticism of Mary Potter Engel (in the Introduction), who attempts to comprehend all the apparent contradictions in Calvin within her "perspectivalist" approach. The approach can perhaps illuminate some difficult points, but it is unsatisfactory when (as I think happens) it conceals defective features of Calvin's thought that need to be faced and straightened out.

16. It may be noted at this point that Turretin avoids Calvin's second inconsistency (between a maximalist concept of the created will and a minimalist concept of the fallen will) by seeking a minimalist view of the will for both states (10.3–4). His consistency lies only on the surface, however, when it becomes evident that he conceals a maximalist view of the created will's freedom under the concept of mutability (see chapter 2, n. 4).

17. *Nicomachean Ethics* 1114b–1115a. The passage concludes Aristotle's discussion of responsibility in Book 3.5.

18. I leave aside here two difficult questions: first, how a single act like the disobedience of our first parents (rather than a series of repeated acts, as in the Aristotelian account cited above) was sufficient to establish our corrupted character and second, how this bondage of sin, together with responsibility for it, is transmitted from the primal couple to the race.

19. Just how such an account is to be properly qualified will be explained in chapter 5 below.

20. Though not pointless for the purpose of maintaining the will's inexcusability for its choice of self against God. This, of course, is an important feature of the fallen state that has to be retained; but it can be, as I show later on in the remedy I propose.

Chapter 4

1. Leith, "Doctrine of the Will," 61.

2. *John's Gospel*, 53, 8, *Nicene and Post-Nicene Fathers,* vol. 7, ed. P. Schaaf (Grand Rapids: Eerdmans, 1956), 293–94.

3. Battles suggests that Calvin is referring here to Erasmus in his treatise against Luther on free will (*Institutes*, 256, n. 4).

Chapter 5

1. Lane seems to accept Calvin's bid to turn the issue into a verbal one, "Did Calvin Believe in Free Will?" 79ff. Turretin does not follow Calvin here, except to warn against a mistaken interpretation of free will that arrogates to human beings an independence from divine authority. Contrary to Calvin, he writes: "Still because it [the term free will] has now been received in the church by a long usage, we do not think it should be dismissed to the philosophers from

whom it seems to have been derived, but should be usefully retained, if its right sense is taught and its abuse avoided" (*Institutes of Elenctic Theology* 10.1.3). But in agreement with Calvin, as we saw earlier, he rejects freedom of contrary choice in favor of freedom of spontaneity as a sufficient analysis of the concept for the fallen state. Like Calvin, he also affirms that the fallen will is, in this sense, freely inclined to nothing but evil (10.4.5,10,38,40; 10.5.9).

2. For a list of passages, see 2.2.17, n. 63.

3. *The Epistles of Paul the Apostle to the Romans and to the Thessalonians*, trans. Ross Mackensie (Grand Rapids: Eerdmans, 1961), 48.

4. Arvin Vos, chapter 6: "Nature and Grace," in *Aquinas, Calvin, and Contemporary Protestant Thought*, especially 142–47; 152–58.

5. For the sophists' view, see Plato's account, *Republic* 2.358–367; for Hobbes, see *Leviathan* 1.13; for Kant, see *The Foundations of the Metaphysics of Morals*, section 1; and for Sartre, see *Being and Nothingness*, 4.1.3; Conclusion.

6. Louis Berkhof, *Systematic Theology* (Grand Rapids: Eerdmans, 1949), 432.

7. Ibid., 434, 436; see also Turretin, *Institutes of Elenctic Theology*, 10.5.

8. The theory of a common, nonsaving grace seems to be original with Calvin and the Reformed tradition. The Medievals were content to explain the virtues and vices of fallen human nature in terms of nature itself as it has been corrupted (though not destroyed) by the fall.

9. Lane says that Calvin's earlier reply to Pighius's charges that he abolished the will in the 1939 edition of the *Institutes* (in his *Reply to Pighius*) "leaves its mark on the 1559 *Institutio*" ("Did Calvin Believe in Free Will?" 82). It is evident, as my analysis shows, that the modifications Calvin introduced in the 1559 edition because of this interchange with Pighius are still inadequate.

10. Francois Wendel says of passages like this one: "After having depicted the spiritual misery of fallen man in the most sombre colours, Calvin now proceeds to paint a much less pessimistic picture of man dealing with his earthly interests. The humanist who was still sleeping within him suddenly awakens, to our surprise" (*Calvin: The Origins and Development of His Religious Thought*, New York: Harper and Row, 1963), 193. Wendel's comment is misleading in its suggestion that Calvin's sombreness on our spiritual condition is owing to his *theology*, his less pessimistic account of our intellectual achievements, to his *humanism*. I have argued that Calvin has as solid a theological basis for the surviving goodness of fallen human nature as he has for its profound spiritual plight, namely, in the doctrine of creation.

11. The phrase "wherever it shall appear" is an echo of Augustine: "Behold where he [God] is; it is wherever truth is found" (*Confessions* 4.12.18; see also 10.24.35).

12. Notice the problems Calvin has trying to affirm consistently the roles of nature and grace in the same human actions in 2.5.13–17.

13. Lane, "Did Calvin Believe in Free Will?" 86.

Epilogue

1. Etienne Gilson, *Christianity and Philosophy* (New York: Sheed and Ward, 1939), 35. The debate continues in various forms today; see, for example, Ralph McInerny's objections to Plantinga's concept of the nature of Christian philos-

ophy in "Reflections on Christian Philosophy," *Rational Faith: Catholic Responses to Reformed Epistemology,* ed. Linda Zagzebski (Notre Dame, Ind.: University of Notre Dame Press, 1993), 256–79.

2. My metaphor is inspired by Plantinga's *The Twin Pillars of Christian Scholarship* (Grand Rapids: Calvin College, 1990). *Twofold* teachings are not foreign to Reformed thinking. Calvin organizes his *Institutes* around the twofold wisdom of self-knowledge and the knowledge of God; or is it, as has also been argued, around the twofold knowledge of God as Creator and as Redeemer? There is also "Divine Sovereignty and Human Responsibility," a commonplace by which Reformed Christians identify the core of their outlook on the world.

3. For a more extensive account, see my *Faith and Reason: An Introduction to Reformed Epistemology,* chapter 6.

4. See chapter 1, n. 2.

5. Plantinga, "Reason and Belief in God," 67–68.

6. Ibid., 18.

7. Ibid., 67, 87.

8. Ibid., 70, 87–91.

9. Ibid., 34.

10. *Rational Faith: Catholic Responses to Reformed Epistemology,* ed. Linda Zagzebski (see n. 1 above). For a more detailed discussion of the points I make here, see my review of Zagzebski's book in *Faith and Philosophy,* 11, 273–81.

11. Zagzebski, *Rational Faith,* 4.

12. Especially interesting voluntarists among the contributors are Thomas D. Sullivan and Patrick Lee (whose work on Scotus I cited in chapter 1).

13. Plantinga, "Reason and Belief in God," 81.

14. Ibid., 34.

15. Ibid., 36.

16. Ibid., 37.

17. Ibid., 37.

18. Ibid., 38.

19. Plantinga has already begun such an account with respect to testimonial beliefs; see *Warrant and Proper Function* (New York: Oxford University Press, 1993), chapter 4; also 183.

20. See note 12 above.

21. "Evidentialism, Plantinga, and Faith and Reason," in *Rational Faith,* ed. Linda Zagzebski, 160.

Works Cited

Ackrill, J. L. *Aristotle the Philosopher.* Oxford: Oxford University Press, 1984.

Aquinas, Thomas. *Summa Theologica. Basic Writings of Saint Thomas Aquinas,* 2 vols. Edited by A. C. Pegis. New York: Random House, 1945.

Aquinas, Thomas. *Summa Theologica,* vol. 13. Translated by the Fathers of the English Dominican Province. London: Oates and Washbourne, 1932.

Aristotle, *Nicomachean Ethics.* Translated by Martin Ostwald. Indianapolis: Bobbs-Merrill, 1962.

Augustine, Aurelius. *Confessions.* Translated by Garden City, N.Y.: Doubleday, 1960.

Augustine, Aurelius. *John's Gospel.* In *Nicene and Post-Nicene Fathers,* vol. 7. Edited by P. Schaaf. Grand Rapids: Eerdmans, 1956.

Augustine, Aurelius. "Predestination of the Saints." In *Basic Writings of St. Augustine.* Edited by W. J. Oates. Chicago: Random House, 1948.

Berkhof, Louis. *Systematic Theology.* Grand Rapids: Eerdmans, 1949.

Bonansea, Bernardine. *Man and His Approach to God in John Duns Scotus.* Lanham, Md.: University Press of America, 1983.

Bourke, Vernon J. *Will in Western Thought.* New York: Sheed and Ward, 1964.

Calvin, John. *The Bondage and Liberation of the Will: A Defense of the Orthodox Doctrine of Human Choice against Pighius.* Edited by A. N. S. Lane and translated by G. I. Davies. Grand Rapids: Baker Books, 1996.

Calvin, John. *The Epistles of Paul the Apostle to the Romans and to the Thessalonians.* Translated by Ross Mackensie. Grand Rapids: Eerdmans, 1961.

Calvin, John. *Institutes of the Christian Religion,* 2 vols. Translated by F. L. Battles. Philadelphia: Westminster, 1960.

Cooper, John. *Body, Soul, and Life Everlasting.* Grand Rapids: Eerdmans, 1989.

Davidson, Donald. "How Is Weakness of the Will Possible?" In *Essays on Actions and Events.* Oxford: Clarendon Press, 1980.

Descartes, Rene. *Discourse on Method* and *Meditations.* Indianapolis: Hackett, 1980.

Descartes, Rene. *Principles of Philosophy; The Passions of the Soul.* In *The Philosophical Works of Descartes.* Translated by E. S. Haldane & G. R. T. Ross. New York: Dover, 1931.

Dihle, Albrecht. *The Theory of Will in Classical Antiquity.* Berkeley: University of California Press, 1982.

Donagan, Alan. "Thomas Aquinas on Human Action." In *The Cambridge History of Later Medieval Philosophy.* Edited by N. Kretzmann, A. Kenny, and J. Pinboorg. Cambridge: Cambridge University Press, 1982.

Dooyeweerd, Herman. *In the Twilight of Western Thought.* Philadelphia: Presbyterian and Reformed Publishing Co., 1960.

Dooyeweerd, Herman. *Transcendental Problems of Philosophic Thought*. Grand Rapids: Eerdmans, 1948.

Engel, Mary Potter. *John Calvin's Perspectival Anthropology*. Atlanta: Scholars Press, 1988.

Gilson, Etienne. *Christianity and Philosophy*. New York: Sheed and Ward, 1939.

Grube, G. M. A. *Plato's Thought*. Indianapolis: Hackett Publishing Co., 1980.

Hare, R. M. *Plato*. New York: Oxford University Press, 1982.

Helm, Paul. *Calvin and the Calvinists*. Edinburgh: The Banner of Truth Trust, 1981.

Hobbes, Thomas. *Leviathan*. Edited by Edwin Curley. Indianapolis: Hackett, 1994.

Hoitenga, Dewey J. Jr. *Faith and Reason From Plato to Plantinga: An Introduction to Reformed Epistemology*. Albany: State University of New York Press, 1991.

Hoitenga, Dewey J. Jr. *Happiness: Goal or Gift?—Two Lectures on the Relationship Between Knowledge, Goodness, and Happiness in Plato and Calvin. The Stob Lectures*. Grand Rapids: Calvin College, 1993–1994.

Hoitenga, Dewey J. Jr., Review of *Rational Faith: Catholic Responses to Reformed Epistemology*. In *Faith and Philosophy* 11 (1995): 283–91.

Kant, Immanuel. *The Foundations of the Metaphysics of Morals*. Trans. L. W. Beck, Indianapolis: Bobbs-Merrill, 1959.

Kendall, R. T. *Calvin and English Calvinism to 1649*. New York and London: Oxford University Press, 1978.

Kenny, Anthony. *The Anatomy of the Soul*. New York: Harper and Row, 1973.

Kenny, Anthony. *Descartes: A Study of His Philosophy*. New York: Random House, 1968.

Kenny, Anthony. *Will, Freedom, and Power*. New York: Harper and Row, 1975.

Lane, A. N. S. "Did Calvin Believe in Free Will?" In *Vox Evangelica* 12 (1981): 72–90.

Lee, Patrick. "The Relation Between Intellect and Will in Free Choice According to Aquinas and Scotus." In *The Thomist* 49 (1985): 321–42.

Lee, Patrick, "Evidentialism, Plantinga, and Faith and Reason," in *Rational Faith: Catholic Responses to Reformed Epistemology*. Edited by Linda Zagzebski. Notre Dame: University of Notre Dame Press, 1993: 140–67.

Leith, John H. "The Doctrine of the Will in the Institutes of the Christian Religion." In *Reformation Perennis*. Edited by B. A. Gerrish and R. Benedetto. Pittsburgh: The Pickwick Press, 1981: 49–66.

Mavrodes, George. "A Futile Search for Sin." In *Perspectives* 8 (January 1993): 9.

Ralph McInerny. "Reflections on Christian Philosophy." In *Rational Faith: Catholic Responses to Reformed Epistemology*. Edited by Linda Zagzebski. Notre Dame, Ind.: University of Notre Dame Press, 1993: 256–79.

Moline, Jon. *Plato's Theory of Understanding*. Madison: University of Wisconsin Press, 1981.

Muller, Richard A. "Fides and Cognitio in Relation to the Problem of Intellect and Will in the Theology of John Calvin." In *Calvin Theological Journal* 25 (1990): 207–24.

Muller, Richard A. "Grace, Election, and Contingent Choice: Arminius's Gambit and the Reformed Response." In *The Grace of God, the Bondage of the Will*, vol. 2. Edited by T. R. Schreiner and B. A. Ware. Grand Rapids: Baker Books, 1995: 251–78.

Parker, T. H. L. *Calvin's Doctrine of the Knowledge of God.* Grand Rapids: Eerdmans, 1959.

Pestana, Mark. "Radical Freedom, Radical Evil and the Possibility of Eternal Damnation," *Faith and Philosophy* 9 (1992): 500–507.

Plantinga, Alvin. *Does God Have a Nature?* Milwaukee: Marquette University Press, 1980.

Plantinga, Alvin. *God, Freedom, and Evil.* New York: Harper Torchbooks, 1974.

Plantinga, Alvin. *God and Other Minds.* Ithaca: Cornell University Press, 1967.

Plantinga, Alvin. *The Nature of Necessity.* Oxford: The Clarendon Press, 1974.

Plantinga, Alvin. "Reason and Belief in God." In *Faith and Rationality: Reason and Belief in God.* Edited by A. Plantinga and N. Wolterstorff. Grand Rapids: Eerdmans, 1983: 16–93.

Plantinga, Alvin. "The Reformed Objection to Natural Theology." In *Proceedings of the American Catholic Philosophical Association* (1980): 49–61.

Plantinga, Alvin. *The Twin Pillars of Christian Scholarship.* Grand Rapids: Calvin College, 1990.

Plantinga, Alvin. *Warrant and Proper Function.* New York: Oxford University Press, 1993.

Plantinga, Cornelius. *Not the Way It's Supposed to Be.* Grand Rapids: Eerdmans, 1995.

Plato. *Republic.* Translated by G. M. A. Grube. Indianapolis: Hackett. 1992.

Ross, W. D. *Aristotle.* New York: Meridian, 1960.

Sartre, John-Paul. *Being and Nothingness.* New York: Philosophical Library, 1992.

Shakespeare, William. *Julius Caesar.* In *Shakespeare: Twenty Three Plays and the Sonnets.* Edited by T. M. Parrott. New York: Scribners, 1938: 634–66.

Smedes, Lewis. *Mere Morality.* Grand Rapids: Eerdmans, 1982.

Stump, Eleonore. "Intellect, Will, and the Principle of Alternative Possibilities." In *Christian Theism and the Problems of Philosophy.* Edited by Michael Beaty. Notre Dame: University of Notre Dame Press, 1990: 254–85.

Taylor, A. E. *Plato: The Man and His Work.* New York: World Publishing Co., 1964.

Torrance, Thomas F. *Calvin's Doctrine of Man.* Grand Rapids: Eerdmans, 1957.

Turretin, Francis. *Institutes of Elenctic Theology*, vol. 1. Translated by G. M. Giger and edited by J. T. Dennison, Jr. Phillipsburg, N.J.: Presbyterian and Reformed Publishing Company, 1992.

Vos, Arvin. *Aquinas, Calvin, and Contemporary Protestant Thought.* Washington D.C. and Grand Rapids: Christian University Press and Eerdmans, 1985.

Walsh, J. J. *Aristotle's Conception of Moral Weakness.* New York: Columbia University Press. 1963.

Wendel, Francois. *Calvin The Origins and Development of His Religious Thought.* New York: Harper and Row, 1963.

Westphal, Merold. "Taking Sin Seriously: Sin as an Epistemological Category." In *Christian Philosophy.* Edited by Thomas Flint. Notre Dame, Ind.: University of Notre Dame Press, 1990: 200–226.

Wolter, Alan. *The Philosophical Theology of John Duns Scotus.* Edited by Marilyn Adams. Ithaca: Cornell University Press, 1990.

Zabzebski, Linda, ed. *Rational Faith: Catholic Responses to Reformed Epistemology.* Notre Dame: University of Notre Dame Press, 1993.

Index

Dewey J. Hoitenga, Jr. is professor of philosophy at Grand Valley State University and author of *Faith and Reason from Plato to Plantinga: An Introduction to Reformed Epistemology*. His Ph.D. degree is from Harvard.